Your Happy Healthy Pet™

Bichon Frise

2nd Edition

GET MORE!
Visit www.wiley.com/
go/bichon-frise

Liz Palika

Howell
Book House™

Copyright © 2006 by Wiley Publishing, Inc., Hoboken, New Jersey. All rights reserved.

Howell Book House
Published by Wiley Publishing, Inc., Hoboken, New Jersey

For general information on our other products and services or to obtain technical support please contact our Customer Care Department within the U.S. at (800) 762-2974, outside the U.S. at (317) 572-3993 or fax (317) 572-4002.

Wiley also publishes its books in a variety of electronic formats. Some content that appears in print may not be available in electronic books. For more information about Wiley products, please visit our web site at www.wiley.com.

Library of Congress Cataloging-in-Publication Data:
Palika, Liz, 1954–
Bichon frise / Liz Palika.—2nd ed.
   p. cm. — (Your happy healthy pet)
ISBN-13: 978-1-63026-059-0

1. Bichon Frise. I. Title. II. Series.
SF429.B52P34 2006
636.72--dc22   2005034540

Printed in the United States of America

10 9 8 7 6 5 4 3 2 1

2nd Edition

Book design by Melissa Auciello-Brogan
Cover design by Michael J. Freeland
Illustrations in chapter 9 by Shelley Norris and Karl Brandt
Book production by Wiley Publishing, Inc. Composition Services

About the Author

Liz Palika is an award-winning author and a well-respected dog trainer. Her work has been published in all the major pet magazines, including *DogWorld*, *Dog Fancy*, *AKC Gazette*, *Cats*, *Cat Fancy*, *Dogs USA*, *Puppies USA*, and others. Her work has also appeared in mainstream publications such as *Newsweek*, *The Saturday Evening Post*, and *Women First*. The author of more than forty-five books, *Save That Dog!* won a Maxwell Award from the Dog Writers Association of America and the first ASPCA Pet Overpopulation Award. Her dog training book, *All Dogs Need Some Training*, was named one of the ten best training books available to dog owners by *Pet Life* magazine.

Liz is the owner of Kindred Spirits Dog Training in Southern California, where she teaches family pet obedience classes, as well as noncompetitive agility and therapy dog training. She was a founding member of the Association of Pet Dog Trainers and of the International Association of Canine Professionals.

About Howell Book House

Since 1961, Howell Book House has been America's premier publisher of pet books. We're dedicated to companion animals and the people who love them, and our books reflect that commitment. Our stable of authors—training experts, veterinarians, breeders, and other authorities—is second to none. And we've won more Maxwell Awards from the Dog Writers Association of America than any other publisher.

As we head toward the half-century mark, we're more committed than ever to providing new and innovative books, along with the classics our readers have grown to love. This year, we're launching several exciting new initiatives, including redesigning the Howell Book House logo and revamping our biggest pet series, Your Happy Healthy Pet™, with bold new covers and updated content. From bringing home a new puppy to competing in advanced equestrian events, Howell has the titles that keep animal lovers coming back again and again.

Contents

Shopping List

You'll need to do a bit of stocking-up before you bring your new dog or puppy home. Below is a basic list of some must-have supplies. For more detailed information on the selection of each item below, consult chapter 5. For specific guidance on what grooming tools you'll need, review chapter 7.

☐ Food dish   ☐ Crate

☐ Water dish   ☐ Nail clippers

☐ Dog food   ☐ Grooming tools

☐ Leash   ☐ Chew toys

☐ Collar   ☐ Toys

☐ ID tag

There are likely to be a few other items that you're dying to pick up before bringing your dog home. Use the following blanks to note any additional items you'll be shopping for.

☐ _____

☐ _____

☐ _____

☐ _____

☐ _____

☐ _____

☐ _____

☐ _____

☐ _____

☐ _____

☐ _____

☐ _____

Pet Sitter's Guide

We can be reached at (___)_____-_____ Cellphone (___)_____-_____

We will return on _____ (date) at _____ (approximate time)

Dog's Name _____

Breed, Age, and Sex _____

Important Names and Numbers

Vet's Name _____ Phone (___)_____- _____

Address _____

Emergency Vet's Name _____ Phone (___)_____- _____

Address _____

Poison Control _____ (or call vet first)

Other individual to contact in case of emergency _____

Care Instructions

In the following three blanks let the sitter know what to feed, how much, and when; when the dog should go out; when to give treats; and when to exercise the dog.

Morning _____

Afternoon _____

Evening _____

Medications needed (dosage and schedule) _____

Any special medical conditions _____

Grooming instructions _____

My dog's favorite playtime activities, quirks, and other tips _____

Part I
The World of the Bichon Frise

The Bichon Frise

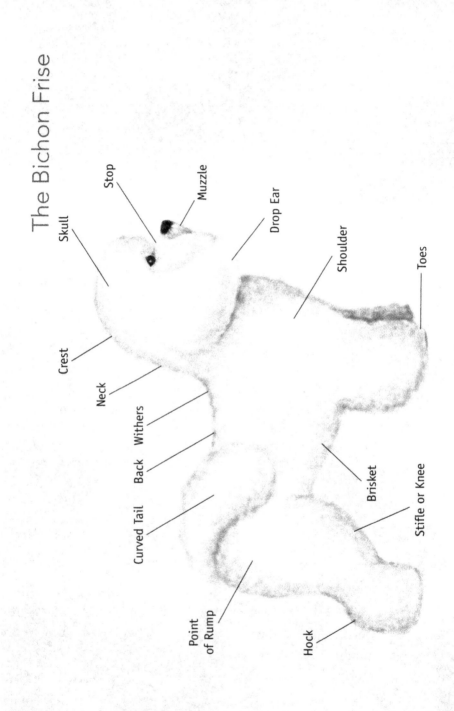

Chapter 1

What Is a Bichon Frise?

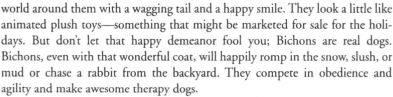

Bichons are fluffy, as white as can be, and react to the world around them with a wagging tail and a happy smile. They look a little like animated plush toys—something that might be marketed for sale for the holidays. But don't let that happy demeanor fool you; Bichons are real dogs. Bichons, even with that wonderful coat, will happily romp in the snow, slush, or mud or chase a rabbit from the backyard. They compete in obedience and agility and make awesome therapy dogs.

Bichons can live happily in a downtown high-rise, a suburban home, or a rural farmhouse. What's important to the dog is his family; Bichons enjoy the company of people. A Bichon Frise should never be a backyard dog, left alone outside for hours at a time, but instead should live in the house with his owners.

For people who want to share their lives with a canine shadow, a Bichon may be the ideal dog. Bichons are great snugglers and will cuddle up close as you read or watch the television, yet are always ready to chase a ball or play with a toy. Bichons are sturdy enough to enjoy long walks and are great ice breakers; it's virtually impossible to go for a walk with a Bichon without at least one person interrupting you with, "What a cute little dog!" A Bichon Frise is a very social, active, versatile, and loyal companion.

What Is a Breed Standard?

A breed standard is a detailed description of the perfect dog of that breed. Breeders use the standard as a guide in their breeding programs, and judges use it to evaluate the dogs in conformation shows. The standard is written by the national breed club, using guidelines established by the registry that recognizes the breed (such as the AKC or UKC).

The first section of the breed standard gives a brief overview of the breed's history. Then it describes the dog's general appearance and size as an adult. Next is a detailed description of the head and neck, then the back and body, and the front and rear legs. The standard then describes the ideal coat and how the dog should be presented in the show ring. It also lists all acceptable colors, patterns, and markings. Then there's a section on how the dog moves, called *gait*. Finally, there's a general description of the dog's temperament.

Each section also lists characteristics that are considered to be faults or disqualifications in the conformation ring. Superficial faults in appearance are often what distinguish a pet-quality dog from a show or competition-quality dog. However, some faults affect the way a dog moves or his overall health. And faults in temperament are serious business.

You can read all the AKC breed standards at www.akc.org.

What Does a Bichon Look Like?

People recognize many breeds of dogs by their appearance. The Rottweiler's distinctive head size and shape, along with the black and copper markings, identify him as a Rottweiler. A German Shepherd's upright ears, black saddle, and tan or red background coat tell people exactly what breed of dog he is. Although personality, temperament, intelligence, and character are always important, the dog's physical appearance conveys that important first impression.

He may look like a little plush toy, but the Bichon Frise is all dog.

This section will provide a brief description of the ideal Bichon Frise, based on the breed standard. For the complete, official breed standard, go to The Bichon Frise Club of America web site (www.bichon.org).

The First Thing You See

When you first see a Bichon, the dog's fluffy white coat strikes your eye. Although there are many white breeds and several fluffy breeds, there is nothing quite like a Bichon. The coat is very white, although occasionally a coat may have some cream, gray, or apricot hairs.

That plush coat is called a *double coat*. That means the outer hairs and the hairs closer to the skin (called *undercoat*) have different textures. The Bichon's outer coat is slightly coarser than the finer, silky undercoat. The coat is slightly curled. The coat is normally brushed out so that it stands out from the body (rather than lying close to the skin). It is then trimmed with scissors to create a rounded shape.

Male Bichons stand nine to twelve inches tall at the top point of the shoulders (called the *withers*), and females are usually nine to eleven inches tall. Most Bichons weigh between seven and twelve pounds. The body is slightly longer than it is tall, and should give the impression of sturdiness without looking heavy or clumsy.

The Head and Expression

One of the hallmarks of the Bichon is the breed's dark-eyed, inquisitive, expressive face. Although they look like stuffed toys, Bichons are not passive or slow thinking; these are bright, intelligent, fun-loving dogs, and those traits should show in each dog's individual expression.

The eyes are black or dark brown, round, and set in the skull to face forward rather than more toward the side, as in some other breeds. The ears are covered with long, flowing coat and hang down (called *drop ears*). The ears are set on the head slightly higher than eye level and more forward, so when the dog is alert, they frame the face.

The nose is prominent, always black, and is not pointed or snippy. The muzzle is balanced to the head, and the lips are black, fine, and never drooping. The Bichon's jaws should meet in a scissors bite, with the outer edges of the bottom front teeth just touching the inner edges of the top front teeth.

The coat on the head is trimmed to create a rounded look, with the ears (and coat on the ears) included in the roundness. The ears should not stand out from the trimmed coat.

The Body, Legs, and Tail

Bichons love to play ball, chase rabbits, climb obstacles, and hurdle small jumps. To do all these things, a Bichon's body and legs must be well muscled and sturdy, yet at the same time the breed should not be overly muscled. A Bichon is all about balance.

The neck is long and arched, and carries the head erect. The neck flows into the shoulders and back, and the topline of the back is level. The chest is well developed and wide enough to allow free movement of the front legs. The chest extends to the point of the elbow of the front legs. There is a slight tuck up (the waist).

The legs are of medium bone and straight with no bow or curve in the forearm or wrist. The feet are round, like a cat's, and point directly forward. The pads are black. The tail is well plumed and carried happily over the back, with the plumes of the tail touching the back. When moving at a trot, the Bichon should appear to move effortlessly.

The Coat

The texture of the Bichon's coat is very important. The undercoat should be soft and dense, and the outer coat is a bit coarser and slightly curlier. The combination of the two coats produces a dense, springy coat. The coat, when bathed and brushed, should stand out from the body, creating a powder puff appearance.

The Bichon should have an inquisitive, expressive face with dark eyes.

The coat should be trimmed to follow the outlines of the body and be rounded off. The head is trimmed to create a round head. The coat should never be trimmed to create a look of squareness. The plumes of the tail are allowed to grow longer than the hair on the body, so the tail plumes flow as the dog moves.

The Bichon's coat is one of its most identifying features, and the correct coat is very important. However, just as the foundation of a house is necessary for the stability of the structure as a whole, the Bichon's correct structure (bones and muscles) are necessary for a sound, balanced, correct dog. Although trimming the coat may seem to hide incorrect structure, an expert can touch the dog, feel under the coat, and identify those faults.

The Bichon's Character

People who see Bichons usually refer to them as "cute," and the breed certainly is incredibly attractive. Bichon owners, however, will stress the breed's temperament more than its physical attributes. Bichons are intelligent, alert, inquisitive, and cheerful. They are gentle and patient with children (as long as the kids are gentle with the dog!), and they are tolerant with other pets. At the same time, Bichons are loud watchdogs.

Friends and Companions

When you are loved by a Bichon Frise, there should be no doubt whatsoever in your mind that you are loved. Bichons love their people, both their family and their friends, and greet their people with a wiggling tail and happy smile every time. It doesn't matter whether you've been gone for an hour or a year; you will be greeted enthusiastically in either case. Bichons never forget a friend.

They are devoted family dogs and will be very tolerant of children's antics as long as the kids are not too rough. Bichons are sturdy for their size but will not tolerate rough handling, especially if the dog decides he's been treated unfairly. Although the breed is not known for snapping or biting, a Bichon who has been treated roughly may snap at the hand that is hurting him, so children must be taught proper behavior around dogs.

Bichons are adaptable companions. If you need some quiet time, they are more than willing to snuggle up by your side. But when you're ready to move, a Bichon will be there, ready for a game of fetch or a brisk walk. If you're feeling down, a Bichon is great therapy, snuggling close and providing all the affection you need.

Alert Watchdogs

Although Bichons are small and cute, they do have a serious side. At home, a Bichon will bark when anyone approaches the house. If the person is identified as family or friend, the bark will turn to cries of joy, but if the person is not recognized, the barking will continue until you relieve the dog of his responsibility or the stranger leaves.

A Bichon is not big enough to be able to actually protect you, your family, or your property and should never be considered a guard dog. An intruder could severely injure a Bichon quite easily. However, an alert, barking dog (no matter what the size) can deter some intruders; they would prefer a quieter place to practice their "skills!"

Most people who own dogs enjoy a warning system such as this. You always know when someone is approaching the house, but it can have its downside, too. Although Bichons are rarely problem barkers, they can take their watchdog duties too seriously. Neighbors do not always appreciate a Bichon's vigor! During their training, all Bichons should learn a command that means, "Thank you for warning me, but that's enough now. Quiet!"

Intelligence and Trainability

Bichons are very intelligent dogs and quickly learn to think through and solve problems. They can open cupboard doors, jump on the dining room chairs, and even open purses left within reach. Luckily, the breed is small; if they were larger they would get into more trouble.

Bichons also have a stubborn streak that is augmented with a little bit of independence. They are not adverse to doing things their own way or ignoring your requests, especially if they're having fun.

Luckily, most Bichons also want to please their owners. This desire to please, combined with the breed's intelligence, means training should be a part of every young Bichon's life. Training should be positive and fun, yet with rules that must be followed. If you are not recognized as the one in control, a Bichon's natural independence may take over—causing innumerable relationship problems later.

Bichons are versatile, trainable companions.

Versatile Companions

Bichons have had an interesting history (as you will read about in the next chapter), but today they are at their best as companion dogs. They love to be with their people. But the term *companion dog* doesn't mean stuck on the couch. No, Bichons are also quite versatile.

Bichon Frises love to walk and will walk with you in your neighborhood, down along the beach, or at the local park. If you like a little more activity, they love to play on an agility course, climbing, jumping, and running over a variety of obstacles. If you are naturally competitive, Bichons have done well in obedience competition. They are also making a mark in the new sport of rally-O.

Bichons are also excellent therapy dogs. Their cute looks make people smile and their affectionate nature warms people's hearts. Bichons are regular visitors in hospitals, nursing homes, day-care centers, and schools.

Chapter 2

The Bichon Frise Yesterday and Today

Archeologists agree that dogs were the first animals domesticated by humans, even before cattle, goats, or horses. Cave drawings from the Paleolithic era, the earliest part of the Old World Stone Age (50,000 years ago) show men and dogs hunting together. Dogs gave warnings of trespassers or enemies. Over time, dogs performed other jobs, including pulling or carrying loads, herding livestock, and more. Although it's hard to compare today's fluffy white Bichons with those ancient, hard-working dogs, today's dogs did all descend from them.

Origins of the Bichon Frise

One school of thought is that the Bichon originated on the island of Malta, off of Spain—the product of mixes between the Maltese, Miniature Spaniel, and Miniature Poodle. Others believe the Bichon is a descendant of the Barbet, a water spaniel with a curly or "frizzy" coat from the Mediterranean.

Although the early origins are not precisely known, most Bichon fanciers accept that the ancestors of today's Bichon Frise arrived on the European continent in the fourteenth century with sailors who brought them to use as barter goods.

In Europe, four variations of this early dog developed: the Bichon Maltese, the Bichon Bolognese, the Tenerife Bichon, and the Bichon Havanese. Although these groups share a common ancestry, they are distinct breeds.

Today's Bichon Frise is the product of mixes between the Maltese, Miniature Spaniel, and Miniature Poodle. You can see the resemblance between this Bichon (second from the right) and her Maltese cousins.

A combination of these Bichon breeds eventually formed the Bichon Frise, although we will never know in what proportions. This makes it difficult to determine the exact origins of the Bichon Frise, but we do know that the Bichon's ancient roots can be traced back to the era before Christ, and that at various times throughout its history, this breed and its predecessors have been desired companions.

The Royal Treatment

At the time of the Renaissance in Europe, the French aristocracy was fascinated with Italian art and culture. Scholars, craftsmen, Italian artifacts, and artists made their way to the French courts. The Bichon, too, was a fashionable trend. The little dog became a pampered pet of the royal family and those with the greatest wealth.

The king and ladies of the court carried these tiny dogs by placing them in baskets attached around their necks by colorful ribbons. It is said that King Henry III of France (who reigned from 1574 to 1589) was never without the company of his Bichons. This may sound a bit too *froufrou*, but in the French court, the more lace, satin, bows, curls, ribbons, and perfume, the better. In fact, the French verb *bichonner* means "to pamper," or "to make beautiful."

The Bichon in Art

It is not unusual to find a small, white, curly-coated dog in portraits done by the old masters. Most of these dogs are shown with more apricot coloring than our ice-white Bichons of today. And, of course, the grooming and trimming done today is much different. However, those dogs were obviously companions and were portrayed close to people, usually touching people and often being petted.

Some of the famous portraits of Bichons were painted by Sir Joshua Reynolds (1746–1792), Francisco Goya (1746–1828), and Emile Carolus-Duran (1838–1917). This is most certainly proof that Bichons were the beloved companions of the rich and famous and also helps substantiate their presence in various historical periods.

A wonderful resource of Bichon-type dogs in artwork from the fifth century B.C. through the twentieth century was compiled by Edward J. Shephard Jr. in The Bichon Frise in Art. This online exhibition has been wonderfully researched and documented and is a great historical resource. You will find it at bingweb.binghamton.edu/~eshephar/bichoninart/bichoninart.html.

Life on the Streets

At the time of the French Revolution, the Bichon began to lose her favored position—as the nobility was losing theirs—and by the nineteenth century, these pampered pets were exiled to the streets to fend for themselves.

For some dogs, this would be the end, but not so the Bichon! Because of their personalities, they made wonderful circus dogs—quick of mind, sturdy, agile, trusting, and loving. There are also stories of gypsies traveling with these small dogs who could smile and perform clever tricks. As street dogs, forced to survive on their own, they quickly learned that life was much easier if they were agreeable and friendly to the world in general. A little smile could go a long way. The Bichon's experience as a circus dog and street performer is perfectly suited to the breed's eager-to-please disposition.

The Bichon in Modern France

In the early twentieth century, there were a few dog fanciers who recognized the potential of these dogs and started to establish their own purebred lines. At the time, the dogs were known by two different names: the Tenerife Bichon and the Bichon à Poil Frisé. On March 5, 1933, the French standard for the breed was approved by the Societe Central Canine de France. It was written by Madame Bouctovagniez, president of the Toy Club of France. The name chosen was Bichon à Poil Frisé (it means "Bichon with the curly coat").

Unfortunately, the breed was severely diminished by the hardships of World Wars I and II. However, as has happened in Europe previously in times of hardship, unregistered dogs were allowed to be used as breeding stock to save the Bichon Frise from extinction. In fact, unregistered dogs were used as breeding stock in regions of Europe up until the early 1970s.

The Bichon in the United States

In October 1956, Mr. and Mrs. Francois Picault of Dieppe, France, came to the United States with several Bichons. Although they exhibited their cute white dogs in rare breed shows, popularity was slow to build. Fortunately, in 1961, Gertrude Fournier, of San Diego, California, became enchanted with the breed. A former Collie breeder, she was wise to the ways of the dog world and was able to help the breed move forward.

Fun-loving little Bichons have done very well in agility in the United States.

What Is the AKC?

The American Kennel Club (AKC) is the oldest and largest pure-bred dog registry in the United States. Its main function is to record the pedigrees of dogs of the breeds it recognizes. While AKC registration papers are a guarantee that a dog is pure-bred, they are absolutely not a guarantee of the quality of the dog—as the AKC itself will tell you.

The AKC makes the rules for all the canine sporting events it sanctions and approves judges for those events. It is also involved in various public education programs and legislative efforts regarding dog ownership. More recently, the AKC has helped establish a foundation to study canine health issues and a program to register microchip numbers for companion animal owners. The AKC has no individual members—its members are national and local breed clubs and clubs dedicated to various competitive sports.

The Bichon's popularity in the United States grew by leaps and bounds. They were shown in rare breed matches, and local clubs were quickly being formed throughout the country. You might say that America was falling in love with the Bichon Frise!

The Bichon Frise Club of America was formed in May 1964, with the help and efforts of Fournier, Azalea Gascoigne, Mayree Butler, Jean Rank, and Goldie Olson. The standard was adopted when the Bichon Frise Club of America was formed. It was modified in 1979 and again in 1988. These modifications were mostly word changes to help breeders and judges better understand and interpret the meaning.

On September 1, 1971, the American Kennel Club permitted the Bichon Frise to compete in the Miscellaneous Class at AKC dog shows. In 1972, the Bichon was officially admitted to the American Kennel Club Stud Book, which is the official record of a dog's registration with the AKC. In 1973, the breed was given full recognition by the AKC and is now shown in the Non-Sporting Group.

The Bichon Today

The Bichon Frise today is the same affectionate, intelligent, cheerful dog she ever was. The fluffy white coat first attracts one's eye, but the wonderful personality cements the relationship. A versatile companion, a Bichon thrives on training and loves to be active.

Bichons have earned AKC championship titles as well as numerous titles at all levels in obedience. In one year, more than 120 Bichons had earned agility titles. Numerous other Bichons have been serving faithfully as therapy dogs. Once you've been loved by a Bichon, all other dog breeds suffer in comparison.

Chapter 3

Why Choose a Bichon Frise?

Happy, fun-loving, and incredibly cute, today's Bichon Frise is a sturdy yet small dog who wants to please you. Intelligent, confident, and not at all shy, the Bichon is ready to conquer the world as long as you're right there by his side. Inquisitive and playful, the Bichon views everything around him as a playground. Bichons thrive with training, too, and learn quickly as long as the trainer is fair and praises a job well done.

But the Bichon is not for everyone. Some people prefer to have a dog who is less animated or more compliant (without that Bichon stubborn streak). Other people would prefer a breed with less coat care.

Are You Ready for a Dog?

Adding a dog to your household, even a small dog, should be a well thought-out decision. You will be taking on the responsibility of a living, thinking, caring creature who will look to you for his happiness and his physical well-being. A dog should never be acquired as an impulse; there is too much at stake. It's always best to think through the repercussions of owning a dog and be honest with yourself. It's too hard on the dog (and you!) if you add a dog to your family and then decide later it was a mistake. So let's take a look at dog ownership first and see if it's right for you, and then we'll see if Bichons are the right breed for you and your family.

First of all, do you have time for a dog? Dogs take a lot of time. They need your companionship and affection, which means you must spend time with them. Dashing in the door, tossing down some dog food, and taking off again are not sufficient. You need to spend time with a dog walking, playing, grooming, training, and just cuddling. A dog is happiest when he can be with his person.

Do you live in a place where a dog can live happily? Are dogs allowed? Will your neighbor complain? Is there a place where a dog can run and play? Unfortunately, not all neighborhoods are dog friendly.

Will you be living alone with the dog or are there roommates or other family members? Does everyone want the dog? If you want a dog but other people in the house do not, that can be very difficult for all concerned. It would be especially difficult for the dog if someone treats the dog badly because they don't want him in the house.

Is there someone in the house who may have some difficulty with the dog? Perhaps a baby, young kids, or a senior citizen? Although these people might enjoy the dog, their abilities should be taken into consideration when you decide on a dog.

Have you lived with a dog before? Do you know what to expect? You may want to borrow a friend's dog for a weekend and see if this lifestyle change is going to be something you'll be happy with.

Are you a meticulous housekeeper? Do you hate it when people track in dirt on their shoes? It's tough to be happy with a dog in the house if you're worried about muss and fuss. Dogs do track in dirt, and they carry in sticks and leaves. Bichons are not tall, but a wagging tail can still knock over knickknacks on a low table or shelf, and puppies will eagerly chew on magazines. Before you bring home a dog, make sure you can live with the mess a dog will make.

This last point may seem overly personal and perhaps not politically correct, but can you afford a dog? This is certainly not the type of thing most people want to talk about, but it is reality. A dog will be another family member who will need things—things you will have to buy. The average cost for the first year of a puppy's life is between $2,000 and $3,000. That includes the dog's purchase price, needed supplies, vaccinations, dog food, spaying or neutering, and all the other miscellaneous expenses. Dog ownership is not cheap.

But dog ownership is wonderful. You will never have a friend as loyal, devoted, and affectionate as a dog. So make sure you're ready for a dog first, and if you are, keep reading.

You'll never have a friend as loyal as a dog.

The Pet Bichon

Although Bichons are watchdogs and will bark vigorously when someone approaches the house, they were never allowed to be aggressive toward people. Bred as companion dogs for hundreds of years, they enjoy the company of people. Today, a correctly bred Bichon is so exuberantly happy (and wiggles so much) upon meeting his people and his people's friends, it almost seems like the front half of his body will detach from the back!

As companions, Bichons should never be isolated to the backyard for hours at a time. Not only are Bichons vulnerable to attack by predators (who are often as prevalent in the cities as they are in rural areas), but this isolation may lead to behavior problems, including nonstop barking, destructive behaviors, and even self-mutilation. Bichons thrive in a household setting, inside with their people.

People of all ages enjoy this breed's charming characteristics. Bichons are active enough for young people who enjoy walking, hiking, playing games, and competing in dog sports. Yet, the breed is also calm enough for older people who enjoy a quieter lifestyle.

Bichons can be very good with children of all ages as long as the kids are gentle with the dog. Bichons do not tolerate rough handling well, and if tormented, will try to get away from the kids first. If that doesn't work, the dog may snap in self-defense. Children should be taught how to handle the Bichon calmly and gently.

This breed is also very tolerant of other pets in the family. Cats and Bichons, if introduced calmly and slowly, can get along quite well and can, in fact, become good friends. Other dogs are fine, too. Bichons are quite social and love to play. If there is a big size difference between dogs, supervise the playtime so the smaller dog doesn't get hurt.

If you have small pets, such as mice, rats, hamsters, or gerbils, keep them away from your Bichon. Although Bichons were bred as companions, many have shown the tendency to hunt small critters, including mice and rats.

Bichons need a lot of grooming. Even if you decide not to keep your dog in a show coat, that curly hair still needs a lot of care.

The Dog's Senses

The dogs eyes are designed so that he can see well in relative darkness, has excellent peripheral vision, and is very good at tracking moving objects—all skills that are important to a carnivore. Dogs also have good depth perception. Those advantages come at a price, though: Dogs are nearsighted and are slow to change the focus of their vision. It's a myth that dogs are color-blind. However, while they can see some (but not all) colors, their eyes were designed to most clearly perceive subtle shades of gray—an advantage when they are hunting in low light.

Dogs have about six times fewer taste buds on their tongue than humans do. They can taste sweet, sour, bitter, and salty tastes, but with so few taste buds it's likely that their sense of taste is not very refined.

A dog's ears can swivel independently, like radar dishes, to pick up sounds and pinpoint their location. Dogs can locate a sound in $6/100$ of a second and hear sound four times farther away than we can (which is why there is no reason to yell at your dog). They can also hear sounds at far higher pitches than we can.

In their first few days of life, puppies primarily use their sense of touch to navigate their world. Whiskers on the face, above the eyes, and below the jaws are sensitive enough to detect changes in airflow. Dogs also have touch-sensitive nerve endings all over their bodies, including on their paws.

Smell may be a dog's most remarkable sense. Dogs have about 220 million scent receptors in their nose, compared to about 5 million in humans, and a large part of the canine brain is devoted to interpreting scent. Not only can dogs smell scents that are very faint, but they can also accurately distinguish between those scents. In other words, when you smell a pot of spaghetti sauce cooking, your dog probably smells tomatoes and onions and garlic and oregano and whatever else is in the pot.

Lots of Coat Care

A big factor that you must take into consideration when deciding whether a Bichon Frise is the right breed for you is the coat. That eye popping, crystal white coat does not remain that way without care—lots of care! The coat must be brushed daily and bathed and trimmed regularly (usually monthly). A coat that is not cared for properly will mat (form big, tangled clumps), and mats must be combed out carefully. If the mat remains, it can damage the skin underneath and will attract debris and parasites. Severely matted dogs often need to be shaved to the skin so that coat can grow out properly. Before adding a Bichon to your home, talk to a friend who owns a Bichon or a professional groomer about the coat care needed by this breed and make sure you're up to the challenge.

The Problem with Popularity

Bichons Frises have become much more popular during the past decade. Although a few years ago the breed was relatively unknown, now they are recognizable everywhere. They have been on television shows, in movies, and in commercials. A Bichon Frise (Ch. Special Times Just Right) even won the prestigious Westminster Kennel Club Dog Show in New York in 2001.

A shy dog may be the result of bad breeding. Bichons should be outgoing and enjoy your company.

Popularity such as this has its good and bad points. For someone who is looking for a Bichon puppy, it's now much easier to find one and more veterinarians, groomers, and trainers are familiar with the breed. That's good.

The bad side is that more Bichons are being produced by people who might not have the breed's best interests at heart. Good breeders are careful to choose animals of fine character and excellent health for breeding stock. Unfortunately, sometimes people breed dogs just for the potential profits and dogs may be produced who are mentally and physically less than ideal. Breeding is an art, and those who decide to breed must educate themselves about both the breed and the genetics of breeding.

The most common trait seen from less-than-ideal breeding is shyness. A Bichon should not be shy; he should be carefree, cheerful, and bold. Shy dogs are usually also fearful, and a fearful Bichon may bite.

Unfortunately, bad Bichons can also be created by their owners. If a young Bichon is neglected, isolated, and not socialized as a puppy, he can become fearful. Some people delight in teasing and tormenting a dog, and although Bichons are very tolerant, even the best Bichons will only take so much.

Unfair or overly harsh discipline can also reduce an outgoing pup to a cowering bundle of nerves. Patience, persistence, and praise are essential when training and raising a young Bichon. Never train or try to discipline a Bichon when you're angry, frustrated, or had a bad day.

If Bichons Could Choose Their Owners

If dogs could choose their owners instead of the other way around, Bichons would probably look for people who enjoy life. Bichons sometimes just dash around the room in celebration of being alive and healthy, and in fact, most Bichons continue to play into old age.

The best Bichon owners are not afraid or embarrassed to play with their dogs. A dog owner can be silly, laugh a lot, and yet still maintain control of both the dog and the situation. Play is wonderful for both the dog and the owner.

Good Bichon owners are also confident. A timid owner can cause a Bichon anxiety. Bichons are not an overly dominant breed, yet someone must be the leader. If the owner isn't in charge and the Bichon would rather not be in charge, that leaves the family rudderless. That's stressful to a dog who craves leadership.

Bichon Frise owners should also enjoy dog training, because every Bichon needs training. Not only does each Bichon need to learn the appropriate social rules, but training teaches you how to train your own dog. When basic obedience class is finished, Bichon owners should look into trick training. Bichons love to do tricks, and because trick training is so much fun, they thrive on it.

Finally, the best Bichon owner loves their dog.

Chapter 4

Choosing Your Bichon Frise

Your new Bichon Frise will be a vital part of your family for the next fourteen to sixteen years, so it's important that you choose your new best friend wisely. Although any dog may fit into your life, when you make a well-researched, educated choice, your chances of success are greatly increased.

The process of choosing the right dog should begin long before you set eyes on any fluffy, fat, appealing puppies. If you wait until you see those puppies, you won't do any research at all. Those babies are too cute and you'll want to take one home right away. But if you want a well-bred, healthy, mentally sound Bichon Frise, you really do need to do some research.

Breeder, Rescue, Shelter, or Free?

You can find a Bichon in many places: from a reputable breeder, a backyard breeder, a Bichon rescue group, your local shelter, or even an ad in the local newspaper. Although the puppy advertised in the newspaper may be the cheapest, and you may get some satisfaction from saving a dog's life at the local shelter, is one of those really the right choice for you? Let's take a look at the pros and cons of each.

Reputable Breeder

A breeder is someone who breeds dogs of a specific breed. In the terminology of dog fanciers, a reputable breeder is someone who knows his breed well, has studied the genetics of the breed, and chooses the sire and dam of each litter carefully.

Reputable breeders usually show their dogs in conformation competition so that judges (who are often also breeders) can evaluate the dogs in their breeding program. Many breeders also compete in other canine sports (obedience, agility, or flyball, for example), so their dogs can use their minds and bodies. Reputable breeders keep up on health issues in the breed, too, and have the necessary health tests done before breeding any dogs.

A reputable breeder screens the people who come to buy one of his puppies because he's concerned about his puppies' future. He may ask you to fill out an application, may ask for references, and will certainly ask you if you've owned dogs before. If you don't sound as if you can provide the right kind of home for one of his puppies, he won't sell you one. Don't take this personally. He's not saying you're a bad person; he's just saying you aren't the right person for his puppies right now.

Many reputable breeders have waiting lists for future litters and if you want one of their puppies, you may have to pay a small deposit and put your name on the waiting list.

If you decide to get a Bichon from a reputable breeder, you will be getting a puppy from someone who will be there for you in the future. He will answer questions for you before, during, and after the purchase of your puppy. You will have been able to meet the mother of the litter and perhaps the father as well. This will give you a good idea of what your puppy will grow up to be in size, coat, and temperament.

The breeder will also begin working with your puppy. The puppy will have been introduced to friendly people and household sounds (such as the dishwasher and the vacuum cleaner), and will have been handled by the breeder since birth so she will be used to human hands. The breeder will also give the puppy her first vaccinations and worming, and will send home instructions for the puppy's care.

Most Bichon breeders keep their puppies until at least 9 to 10 weeks of age. Never bring home a puppy before 8 weeks of age; if the breeder says it's okay, get a puppy from someone else. Puppies, especially tiny puppies, need that extra time with their mother and their litter-mates to grow up mentally and physically healthy.

Never bring home a puppy younger than 8 weeks old. These little ones still have much to learn from their mom and littermates.

Backyard Breeder

A backyard breeder is someone who has bred his dogs but does not have the knowledge (or desire, or energy, or finances) to do what is necessary to produce the best dogs possible. This could be someone who has a female Bichon and, because he wants puppies, he breeds his female to a friend's male down the street. No health checks were done, no studies of genetics or background checks were done, and in many instances the dogs might not have been registered, either.

A backyard breeder may also be someone who hasn't spayed his female Bichon and then doesn't keep her safe when she comes into season and is bred by a wandering male. The puppies may or may not be purebred; the male (or males) may not even be known.

The term *backyard breeder* may also refer to someone who is trying to make money off the breed. He knows the breed is popular right now and just wants to make some quick cash by breeding his pet.

Backyard breeders may produce some nice puppies. It has happened, and the smart backyard breeder will ask for help from an experienced, reputable breeder. But they are just as likely to produce dogs with problems. In addition, once the puppies are born, the backyard breeder rarely knows what the pups need to grow up well, so the pups may not be handled enough or correctly, may not have the socialization they need, and may not have their first sets of shots. Backyard breeders often sell their puppies as soon as they are weaned, which may be between five and six weeks of age; this is much too soon for the pups to leave their mother and littermates. The backyard breeder rarely has a waiting list for his puppies, and as the puppies get older, they are often turned over to the local shelter.

Bichon Frise Rescue

Puppies are a lot of work and not everyone is ready for that commitment. But just because you don't want a puppy doesn't mean you cannot add a Bichon to your family. Very often, adolescent or adult Bichons need new homes. The owner may have passed away, or was transferred overseas, or perhaps the owner made the wrong choice and a Bichon was not the right dog for them.

Purebred rescue groups are organized by national, regional, or local breed clubs (such as The Bichon Frise Club of America), or by people who simply want to aid the breed they love. These people take in Bichons, foster them, evaluate their temperament, get them health care, and then adopt the dogs out to new homes. Purebred rescue groups also sponsor educational activities, usually on a local level, teaching people about their breed of choice.

People wishing to adopt a rescue dog are required to fill out an application and are usually also asked to supply a couple of references. A home inspection is often required, too, so that the rescue group can make sure the home is safe and secure for a small dog.

Although you might not know as much about a rescue dog as you would if you'd have gotten a dog from a reputable breeder, the evaluation process is usually very thorough. You will know whether your dog is healthy and if she has any training or behavioral challenges. Rescue groups are also good about follow ups; if you need help after adopting a dog, someone will be there to help you.

Shelter Bichons

Dogs of all kinds, including Bichons, end up in local shelters for many reasons. Some people buy a Bichon for her appearance and don't understand the breed's temperament. Sometimes the parents neglect to teach their children how to handle a small dog and the dog ends up snapping at the kids. Or perhaps the dog's owner passed away and no one in the family wants the Bichon.

Shelters are as good or as bad as the community that supports them and the people who run them. Some shelters are wonderful. The dogs' runs are kept clean, the dogs are housed well, and they get a lot of attention. Other shelters are horrible.

A dog from a rescue group or a shelter may make a fine pet.

A Bichon in a shelter is an unknown. Kept in a run, often with other small dogs, the Bichon will be incredibly stressed and you won't be able to see her true personality. She may or may not be housetrained, may or may not be good with kids, and may or may not be good with other pets. However, if you can get her out of that run, even for a fifteen-minute walk, you may be able to get a glimpse of who the real dog is inside all that stress.

Many people want to adopt a dog from the shelter because they like the feeling that they are saving a dog's life. That's super, as long as you understand that you're getting a total unknown. Keep in mind, too, that the first three months after adopting a dog are the honeymoon months. You won't see the "real" dog for at least that long, because it takes that long for the dog to adjust to her new home and family.

Free Bichons

My grandpa had a saying, "If you get something for free, that's exactly what it's worth!" Although a free dog may seem like a bargain (and sometimes she is), she may also be a very expensive mistake. The fluffy puppy in a box outside the grocery store may or may not be a Bichon; she may be a Bichon mix with an unknown father or even a Poodle mix.

The chances are also pretty good that a free puppy has had no vaccinations and was never wormed. In fact, the mother of the litter was probably not vaccinated or wormed, either! Waiting in the box for a new owner, the puppy was probably handled by a number of different people, many of whom have dogs at home. How many of them passed along diseases or germs to the puppy?

You will never know for sure what the parentage of the free puppy is, and you should be skeptical of anything the owner of the puppy says. After all, if the puppies are so wonderful, why are they in a box outside a grocery store? Hmmm?

Finding the Right Bichon

It's not hard to find a Bichon; they are growing in popularity. However, it may not be that easy to find the right dog for you. Don't be in a hurry and don't take the first Bichon you see. Take your time, do some research, and temper your emotions with thought.

When you begin your search, talk to people. Just as networking is a great way to find a job, it's also a great way to find a dog. Ask people if they know of a good Bichon breeder. If you see a beautiful, well-groomed, healthy Bichon walking with her owners, ask the owners where they got their dog. Ask them, too, about that experience: Would they go to that person for their next dog?

Bichon Frise clubs can also be a good place to find breeders. The AKC web site lists local dog clubs. You can also do an Internet search for a club in your area (for example, in a search engine type "Bichon Frise club + your city, county, and state"). Go to a meeting or two, introduce yourself, and tell them you are looking for a Bichon puppy (or young adult). When they learn you're serious about finding a good pet and companion, they will be more than happy to help you. Don't be insulted if people are standoffish initially, though. The people in the club are going to want to see if you're serious about the breed before doing business with you.

After you get a couple of referrals to breeders or rescue groups, call and set up an appointment to meet with each of them. Some may prefer to talk on the phone, but others may invite you out to meet some dogs.

Ask the breeder a few questions: How long have you been breeding? Do you show your dogs? Do your Bichons also compete in any dog sports? What health screenings do you do? What kind of sales contract and guarantee do you offer with a puppy?

You can ask a rescue group volunteer similar questions: Where do the dogs come from? Does the group do any health screening? How long do the dogs stay with a foster home and how much do you know about the dogs being fostered? Are the dogs spayed or neutered? Vaccinated? Microchipped?

Be prepared to answer some questions yourself, as the breeder or rescue group volunteer will want to know something about you, your family, and your home situation. Why do you want a Bichon? Have you ever kept a coated dog?

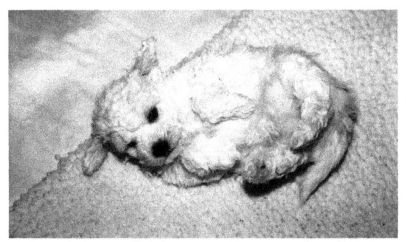

Reputable breeders feel responsible for every puppy they produce and want to make sure all their dogs end up in loving, permanent homes.

Are you prepared to do the necessary grooming? What are your goals for the dog? Have you ever trained a dog before? Where do you live? Do you own your own home or rent? Are dogs allowed? Do you have a securely fenced yard? Your answers to these and other questions may determine whether a breeder will sell you a dog or if a rescue group will let you adopt one.

Choosing the Puppy for You

Bichon puppies, with their fluffy white coat and dark, expressive eyes, are the cutest things on the face of this planet. They are hard to resist. It's impossible to look at a litter of these puppies and not love them all, so how are you supposed to choose just one?

Breeders, dog trainers, and service dog experts have developed puppy tests. These tests enable people to evaluate a puppy's responses to specific stimuli and, as a result, choose puppies who are suited to the purpose at hand. Service dog trainers are able then to focus their time and energies on puppies who are most suited for their work, for example, rather than on puppies who have little chance to succeed. Puppy tests can help pet dog owners, too, because you can then choose the best dog for you, your personality, and your goals for your dog. If you want to do obedience competition in the future, for example, or therapy dog work, you can find the puppy best suited for that work.

These tests are not foolproof, because the dog's owner, trainer, and the environment the puppy lives in still have a great deal to do with how the puppy grows up. But these tests can help increase your chances of finding the right puppy for you.

These tests are best done with Bichons when the puppies are 7 or 9 weeks of age. (Do not do these tests during the fear period that occurs during the eighth week.) Many breeders use these tests, too, so if your dog's breeder does, just ask if you can watch. If he doesn't, ask him if he will allow you to do the test. Most will.

On a sheet of paper, list all the puppies. You can use different color ribbons or collars on the puppies to differentiate them. Red collar, blue collar, green collar, and so on.

Look at the Whole Litter

Without getting involved, watch the litter as a group. By 7 weeks of age, the puppies will be playing with one another, bouncing around clumsily, mock fighting, growling, and barking. Make notes about their behavior. The boldest puppy, who is often (but not always) the biggest, is the first to do anything. She will grab an unfamiliar toy first and be the first to the food bowl. This puppy

Different dogs are right for different families.

will be great for an active person with a matching bold personality but would not be good for someone who lives alone and works long hours or someone who prefers a calm, quiet dog.

The shy, fearful puppy is the one sitting in the corner alone, just watching what's going on. She may duck her head when approached and may look away when spoken to. Although the fearful puppy may come out of her shell with a calm, caring owner, dogs with this temperament may always have the tendency to be afraid. Although Bichons should be happy and confident, a fearful personality is, unfortunately, sometimes seen in the breed.

Most puppies will fall between these two extremes. In one situation, a certain puppy will be bold and outgoing while in another situation, that same pup may fall back and watch. While you're observing, just make notes as to who is the crybaby, who is the instigator, who always gets the toy, and who is first to the food or treats. These notes will help you later.

The Test

Now you're ready for the Puppy Temperament Test in the box on pages 38–39. Have your pad of paper at hand and make notes as you go along, or better yet,

The Puppy Temperament Test

Walk Away

Place a puppy on the ground at your feet. Stand up and walk away. Does the puppy:

A. Follow you.
B. Put herself underfoot, climbing all over your feet.
C. Do a belly crawl to follow you.
D. Ignore you and go in the other direction.

Call the Puppy

Move away from the puppy, bend over, and call her, spreading your hands and arms wide to encourage her. Does the puppy:

A. Come to you, tailing wagging.
B. Chase you so fast you don't have a chance to call her.
C. Come slowly or crawl on her belly to you.
D. Ignore you.

Gentle Restraint

Gently roll the puppy onto her back in your arms and place a hand on her chest. Restrain her this way for thirty seconds—no longer. Does she:

ask the breeder or a friend to make notes for you. Test each puppy individually. Don't go through the scores until you have tested all the puppies.

Looking at the Results

There are no right or wrong answers to these tests. Rather, they are simply a guide to help you choose the right puppy for you. No one has figured out how to accurately foretell the future, but these tests can help us make an educated guess.

The puppy who scored mostly As is a middle-of-the-pack dog in terms of dominance. This is not the most dominant puppy nor the most submissive. If this puppy also scored A in retrieving a ball, this puppy should suit active couples or most families with well-behaved children. This puppy should accept

A. Struggle for a few seconds but then relax.
B. Struggle for the entire thirty seconds.
C. Cry, tuck her tail up, and perhaps urinate.
D. Struggle for fifteen seconds and then stop, look at you, or perhaps look away.

Lifting

When the puppy is on the ground, place both hands under her rib cage and lift her paws off the ground for thirty seconds. Does the puppy:

A. Quietly accept it without struggling.
B. Struggle for at least fifteen seconds.
C. Accept it with a tucked tail, some crying, and perhaps some urinating.
D. Struggle for more than fifteen seconds and try to turn and nip at your hands.

Tossing a Ball

With the puppy close to you, show her a ball and then toss it just a few feet away. Does the puppy:

A. Dash after it, pick it up, and bring it back to you.
B. Bring it back but not want to give it to you.
C. Go after it but not pick it up or get distracted by something else.
D. Pick it up but then walk away.

training well, and although she may have some challenges during adolescence, she should grow up to be a nice dog.

The puppy who scored a mixture of As and Bs will be a little more dominant and will probably challenge a little more during training and as an older puppy. If the puppy scored a B or D on the retrieve, training could be more of a challenge.

The puppy who scored predominantly Bs is a more dominant personality. She could grow up to be a great agility competition dog or a flyball whiz with the right owner. This dog is not good for a person with a soft personality; she will need someone as strong as she is. This dog will need structured training from puppy-hood into adulthood.

The puppy who scored mostly Cs is a more fearful or timid personality. She must be handled carefully, as this puppy could bite if she's pushed too far. She needs a calm

No one can predict exactly how a puppy will turn out, but there are ways to make an educated guess.

environment where she will be encouraged to be more confident but will not be coddled. She also needs a calm, confident owner. This dog would do well in a quiet home with a couple or a single adult. This dog should not be in a home with kids.

The puppy who scored Cs and Ds may have trouble bonding with people, yet when she does bond, she will be devoted and loyal. Cautious and independent, this dog could be a challenge. She needs a calm home where she will be trained using positive yet structured training.

The dog who scored mostly Ds isn't sure she needs people. She is independent and confident, and very sure of herself. She will need to spend lots of time with her owner so she can develop a relationship. She will need an owner who will be a fair yet firm leader.

Listen to Your Heart

After evaluating the scores, set aside those pups who do not suit your needs at all. Now look at the ones remaining. Are there three puppies whose scores suggest they might be right for you? Now you need to listen to your heart. Which of these remaining puppies appeals to you the most? Which ones are you drawn to?

Watch the puppies' reactions to you, too. Is one puppy trying to climb up your legs? Is one staring at you, trying to make eye contact? It's not unusual to have a puppy choose her new owner.

Choosing an Adult Bichon

Choosing an adult dog is both a little easier and a little harder than choosing a puppy. A puppy is the result of her genetics and the care she has received as a baby. She is also all potential—a blank slate waiting for something to be put on it.

An older puppy or an adult is all this, too, but she also has a history. That history could be a loving home where the Bichon was a treasured member of the family or it could be a neglectful home where she was ignored, underfed, and isolated from people. Worse yet, she may have been abused.

The things that have happened to a Bichon before she ended up with a rescue group or in a shelter all have a bearing on her future. If she was mistreated or abused, she may duck every time someone reaches toward her. She may try to run away when she sees a mop or a broom. She may try to bite when a hand reaches toward her collar or she may urinate when someone picks her up.

Although it may seem horrendous that someone could abuse a Bichon, unfortunately, it does happen. Luckily, most Bichons are very forgiving, and although they may continue to hold a grudge against the person who has hurt them, they do not hold a grudge against the entire human race.

When you look at adult Bichons, try to find out as much as you can about the dog before adopting her. Ask the rescue volunteer or shelter personnel as many questions as you can think of: What is her personality like? How does she react to the broom, hose, or mop? Does she duck when people pet her or does she eagerly climb into your lap? Does she appear aggressive (or fearful) toward anything (or anyone) in particular? Is she calm around people of all ages, sizes, shapes, and ethnic backgrounds?

Tests used on baby puppies will not work on adult dogs, so you have to rely more on the information you can get from the people working with the dog. Spend some time with her, ask many questions, and if you can, take her for a few walks. You may also want to see if you can take her home for a weekend on a "test drive" before you decide if she's the right dog for you.

Puppy or adult? They each have their advantages.

Part II

Caring for Your Bichon Frise

Chapter 5

Getting Ready for Your Bichon Frise

Bringing home your new Bichon is very exciting. This is a new family member who will be by your side for the next fourteen to sixteen years. Wow! Think of the good times you will both share, the adventures, and the companionship.

Bringing home a new Bichon puppy or adult can also be very stressful—for you and your dog—so you're going to want to prepare so you can be sure things go as smoothly as they can. You want the adjustment to be as easy as possible and you will need to be ready for anything that may happen.

First, you need to make sure your house and yard are safe for him. Bichons, both puppies and adults, are insatiably curious and will get into things you may not expect. So it's important that you create a safe environment for your new dog. When you first introduce your Bichon into your household, and while he's growing up and learning the rules of the house, you must keep the house, yard, and garage as safe as possible. The box on pages 46–47 explains how.

After all, your dog doesn't know what can hurt him (or even kill him), and you need to teach him his new household rules. You won't have to live this way forever; your dog will learn to live with you without destroying your home. But right now, it's important you keep your new companion safe.

A Secure Dog Yard

Your Bichon Frise is not a backyard dog. Your Bichon is a house dog, living in the house with you and your family. However, that doesn't mean your Bichon won't enjoy spending some time outside. Most Bichons enjoy watching the butterflies and birds fly in and out of the yard and, of course, chasing squirrels and lizards is great fun. Basking in the sun while snoozing is also a favorite canine occupation.

Bichons are small dogs, though, and being outside unsupervised does present some dangers. You need to make sure your Bichon has a safe outdoor space. He shouldn't be able to escape from the yard, and any native predators (four-footed or winged) must be prevented from getting to him. Bichons are small enough to be quite vulnerable.

A dog run is usually much easier to make secure than an entire yard, especially if you have birds of prey in your area (large hawks, turkey vultures, or eagles) that could swoop into your yard for a meal. A dog run could be secure chain-link fencing, with a firm flooring to which the chain link can be fastened at the bottom to keep Bichons in and predators out. The top can be covered with fencing or with a securely fastened tarp.

The dog yard should have unspillable water and shade at all times, and a place where your dog can rest comfortably (a pile of bedding or a dog house). Many people use the dog yard for housetraining, taking the dog to that area each time he needs to go outside to relieve himself.

In any case, your Bichon should not spend all day, every day, in the dog yard. But he certainly can spend a little time here and there.

You'll need to make sure your dog is safe and secure when he's out in the yard.

Puppy-Proofing Your Home

You can prevent much of the destruction puppies can cause and keep your new dog safe by looking at your home and yard from a dog's point of view. Get down on all fours and look around. Do you see loose electrical wires, cords dangling from the blinds, or chewy shoes on the floor? Your pup will see them too!

In the kitchen:

- Put all knives and other utensils away in drawers.
- Get a trash can with a tight-fitting lid.
- Put all household cleaners in cupboards that close securely; consider using childproof latches on the cabinet doors.

In the bathroom:

- Keep all household cleaners, medicines, vitamins, shampoos, bath products, perfumes, makeup, nail polish remover, and other personal products in cupboards that close securely; consider using childproof latches on the cabinet doors.
- Get a trash can with a tight-fitting lid.
- Don't use toilet bowl cleaners that release chemicals into the bowl every time you flush.
- Keep the toilet bowl lid down.
- Throw away potpourri and any solid air fresheners.

In the bedroom:

- Securely put away all potentially dangerous items, including medicines and medicine containers, vitamins and supplements, perfumes, and makeup.
- Put all your jewelry, barrettes, and hairpins in secure boxes.
- Pick up all socks, shoes, and other chewables.

In the rest of the house:

- Tape up or cover electrical cords; consider childproof covers for unused outlets.
- Knot or tie up any dangling cords from curtains, blinds, and the telephone.

- Securely put away all potentially dangerous items, including medicines and medicine containers, vitamins and supplements, cigarettes, cigars, pipes and pipe tobacco, pens, pencils, felt-tip markers, craft and sewing supplies, and laundry products.
- Put all houseplants out of reach.
- Move breakable items off low tables and shelves.
- Pick up all chewable items, including television and electronics remote controls, cellphones, shoes, socks, slippers and sandals, food, dishes, cups and utensils, toys, books and magazines, and anything else that can be chewed on.

In the garage:

- Store all gardening supplies and pool chemicals out of reach of the dog.
- Store all antifreeze, oil, and other car fluids securely, and clean up any spills by hosing them down for at least ten minutes.
- Put all dangerous substances on high shelves or in cupboards that close securely; consider using childproof latches on the cabinet doors.
- Pick up and put away all tools.
- Sweep the floor for nails and other small, sharp items.

In the yard:

- Put the gardening tools away after each use.
- Make sure the kids put away their toys when they're finished playing.
- Keep the pool covered or otherwise restrict your pup's access to it when you're not there to supervise.
- Secure the cords on backyard lights and other appliances.
- Inspect your fence thoroughly. If there are any gaps or holes in the fence, fix them.
- Make sure you have no toxic plants in the garden.

Basic Supplies

You'll need to go shopping *before* you bring home your new Bichon. Obviously, you will need some dog food. We'll talk about this more in the next chapter, but for now, find out what your Bichon is currently eating and have some of that on hand. You don't want to change foods abruptly because that can cause gastrointestinal upset. If you want to change your dog's food later, you can do so gradually.

You will need a food bowl and a couple of water bowls. Although Bichons are not rough like some bigger, stronger breeds, you may want to get unbreakable, unspillable bowls anyway. Bichon puppies have been known to use their water bowls as toys!

Get a collar that closes with a buckle for your puppy. An adjustable one works well because you can make it larger as your puppy grows. Make up an identification tag at your local pet supply store and have a couple of telephone numbers on it (home and cell or home and work). Don't worry if you haven't decided on a name for your new dog; you can make up a new tag later with his name on it. Right now you want to have a way to get your puppy back to you just in case he gets away from you.

A leash is necessary, too, of course. A lightweight nylon or cotton web leash with a small snap on it will work well. Don't put a heavy leash (one inch wide or wider) with a big snap on your Bichon, because it will weigh heavy on his neck. He could develop a dislike for his leash and for walks on the leash.

These giant toys may be fun for the baby, but your Bichon will need toys that are the right size for a little dog.

Puppy Essentials

You'll need to go shopping *before* you bring your puppy home. There are many, many adorable and tempting items at pet supply stores, but these are the basics.

- **Food and water dishes.** Look for bowls that are wide and low or weighted in the bottom so they will be harder to tip over. Stainless steel bowls are a good choice because they are easy to clean (plastic never gets completely clean) and almost impossible to break. Avoid bowls that place the food and water side by side in one unit—it's too easy for your dog to get his water dirty that way.
- **Leash.** A six-foot leather leash will be easy on your hands and very strong.
- **Collar.** Start with a nylon buckle collar. For a perfect fit, you should be able to insert two fingers between the collar and your pup's neck. Your dog will need larger collars as he grows up.
- **Crate.** Choose a sturdy crate that is easy to clean and large enough for your puppy to stand up, turn around, and lie down in.
- **Nail cutters.** Get a good, sharp pair that are the appropriate size for the nails you will be cutting. Your dog's breeder or veterinarian can give you some guidance here.
- **Grooming tools.** Different kinds of dogs need different kinds of grooming tools. See chapter 7 for advice on what to buy.
- **Chew toys.** Dogs *must* chew, especially puppies. Make sure you get things that won't break or crumble off in little bits, which the dog can choke on. Very hard plastic bones are a good choice. Dogs love rawhide bones, too, but pieces of the rawhide can get caught in your dog's throat, so they should only be allowed when you are there to supervise.
- **Toys.** Watch for sharp edges and unsafe items such as plastic eyes that can be swallowed. All dogs will eventually destroy their toys; as each toy is torn apart, replace it with a new one.

A crate will serve as your new Bichon's bed, and we'll discuss that in more detail later in this chapter. You can put some old towels in the crate for bedding. Don't buy an expensive bed or pad right now because your Bichon may chew on it or have a housetraining accident. Some towels that are easy to wash are fine. Later, you can buy that fancy bed.

Your Bichon will need some grooming supplies, and we'll discuss those in chapter 7. Right now, just pick up some gentle dog shampoo, conditioner, a hand-held blow dryer with a gentle heat setting, a slicker brush, and a metal-tooth comb. These grooming tools will serve you well while your puppy is adjusting to your home. You can add grooming supplies as your Bichon grows up and grows more coat, and as you need them.

Your Bichon will also need some toys. Do not give him old socks or shoes because that will teach him to chew on your things and you won't be happy about it when he finds your new, expensive leather shoes. Instead, get him some dog toys. Soft, fuzzy toys are favorites of most Bichons, as are squeaky toys and small balls.

The Great Crate

Dogs like to nap in small, dark, enclosed places. These places, like a wild dog's den, make them feel secure and protected. A crate serves the same purpose for your Bichon. Although some dog owners think of a crate as cruel, in fact a dog sees it as a safe, secure bed with a door. Crates have made thousands of dogs' lives better and helped their owners train them more productively.

In chapter 10 we'll discuss housetraining, and the crate will be a tremendous benefit in that process. In addition, the crate will serve as your Bichon's bed or playpen, so he can be safely confined when you can't watch him.

It's difficult to imagine how much trouble little puppies can get into when they have unlimited freedom in your home. A crate and a pen or baby gates are necessities.

Buy your Bichon a crate that will fit him when he's full grown but don't get one big enough for a Golden Retriever. He should have enough room to stand up, turn around, and lie down comfortably.

Every time you put your Bichon in the crate, toss in a toy or cookie as you tell him, "Sweetie, go to bed!" Praise him when he goes inside. Ignore him if he cries and never, ever let him out when he's throwing a temper tantrum. That rewards the bad behavior! Instead, let him out when he's calm and quiet.

Pet Professionals

You will need several pet professionals to assist you throughout your Bichon's lifetime, and it's easier to find those people before you bring home your Bichon and before you need their help. Don't wait until there is an emergency!

A Veterinarian

A veterinarian will help you keep your Bichon healthy. She will guide you through the vaccination process and spaying and neutering, and will be there if your Bichon has a health problem. You can find a good vet through personal referrals. Ask your dog's breeder. Ask your friends or neighbors where they take their pets and if they are happy with the service that vet provides.

If one local veterinarian's name pops up often, make an appointment to talk to that vet. Be prepared to pay for an office visit (even though you aren't bringing in a dog) because you are taking up her time. Ask the vet several questions: Are you familiar with Bichons? What health problems do you see in the breed? Do you have any difficulties working with the breed? Ask her about her office and payment policies and ask her, too, what her emergency arrangements are.

A Trainer

A dog trainer is also important, especially during puppyhood. A trainer can help you socialize your Bichon, guide you through the housetraining process, and assist you during your Bichon's adolescence.

You can find a dog trainer through referrals, too. When you see a nicely behaved dog (of any breed) walking with his owners, ask them where they went for training. You can also ask local veterinarians where they recommend their clients go for training. Before you sign up, watch a few of this trainer's classes to make sure you would be comfortable with her training style.

With that luxurious coat, a professional groomer will be an important part of your dog's life.

A Groomer

A groomer is going to be very important to you and your dog, unless you're prepared to do all the grooming yourself. Although many Bichon owners will do some of the grooming, very few are prepared or willing to do all of it, especially the haircuts. Again, referrals can send you to a reputable groomer.

Ask some Bichon owners where they take their pets. Grooming a Bichon is not like grooming a Poodle or a terrier, and a Bichon should never look like a Poodle.

Drop by the grooming shop and take a look around. Although a few dogs may be barking when you walk in, it should quiet down soon. The shop will have dog hair floating around and may smell like wet dogs, but otherwise, it should be clean. The dogs should be in dry, clean cages. Ask the groomer if she sees many Bichons and if she does, does she like working with them?

Bringing Home Your Bichon

Okay, you've done your research, you have a Bichon puppy or adult all picked out, and you've gone shopping. Your house and yard are puppy proofed and you have checked out some pet professionals. It's time to bring home your new best friend. Are you ready? Sure you are! This will be a wonderful new adventure.

Plan on bringing your Bichon home when you will be able to stay at home for at least a couple of days. A Friday night is good if you can spend Saturday and Sunday at home. Do not bring home a new dog, go to bed, and then go to work the next morning. That would be very traumatic for the dog.

Don't invite the neighborhood and all your friends over to see your new dog, either. Your dog needs to get used to you, his new house, and the yard, and needs to learn where to go to relieve himself. Too many people will overwhelm him and will slow down the bonding process with you. People can meet your dog next week.

Your Bichon will need to get to know his new home so take him to the area where you want him to relieve himself and praise him when he does. Show him where his water dish is. Show him where his toys will be kept. Introduce him to his crate by tossing a cookie or a toy inside. Don't carry him; let him walk to all these places. He may be tiny, but he is a dog and would prefer to move under his own power.

Start teaching him household rules right from the beginning, too. If you don't want him underfoot in the kitchen, keep him out of the kitchen right from the start. If you are going to allow him up on the sofa but not on the easy chairs, begin enforcing that right away. Teach him and shape him as you would like to see him grow up.

Remember, your new puppy is just a baby and will be overwhelmed by all the new sights and smells at your home. Don't invite your friends and neighbors to meet him until he has had a few days to settle in.

Plan on taking him to the veterinarian's office soon. The contract from your breeder may even state a time period. This is for your protection as well as the breeder's. If there is a health problem, such as a congenital defect, the vet should find it now rather than later. If there is a problem, you can talk to the breeder about it before you get too attached to the puppy. The vet will also want to see what vaccinations your Bichon has already had and set up a schedule for future shots.

Chapter 6

Feeding Your Bichon Frise

Your Bichon Frise needs a good diet to maintain her health. Good nutrition will keep your dog's beautiful coat lush and full. Even more important, it will help prevent many problems and can certainly contribute to a long life.

Dog food is one item where you usually get what you pay for. The cheaper foods (especially the plain label or generic foods) are made of cheaper, lesser quality ingredients and the more expensive foods (premium or super premium) are made from better quality ingredients that offer your dog more nutrition.

The Elements of a Good Diet

A good quality dog food will contain all of the essential elements needed by dogs. Those include proteins, carbohydrates, fats, vitamins, and minerals. These must be supplied in correct proportions so the dog can make use of them.

Proteins

Proteins are found in fish, meat, milk, eggs, cheese, and some beans. They are needed for essential body building, including growth, healing, and the replacement of body tissues burned up by normal activity. Twenty to thirty percent of your dog's meal should be protein, depending on your dog's age and activity level. Growing puppies require extra protein. Protein is not stored, so your Bichon must eat it every day.

Carbohydrates

Carbohydrates are found in grains and other plant parts. Carbohydrates provide energy to the body and aid in digestion and elimination. Some dog foods also use carbohydrates as fillers (to make your dog feel full), and although this may have some use for dogs who need to lose weight, the side effect is that your dog may eat so many fillers that she isn't eating enough protein and fat to get the nutrition she needs.

Fat

Although fats have gotten a bad rap lately, they are important. Dogs do not suffer from heart disease caused by high cholesterol. Fat acts as a vitamin reserve, storing some vitamins until they are needed by the body and then assisting the body in the metabolism of those vitamins. Fats also aid digestion by slowing the passage of food through the intestines. Fats also help keep your Bichon's coat healthy and shiny. Fats provide twice as much energy as an equivalent amount of carbohydrates or protein, but too much fat will cause diarrhea.

Your dog needs a healthy, balanced diet to keep her active and fit.

Vitamins

Vitamins are necessary for life, as they are an integral part of many bodily processes. Vitamin A is necessary for healthy eyesight, reproduction, growth, and many other bodily processes. Vitamin A is also a strong antioxidant, fighting free radicals that could cause cellular damage, especially as your Bichon ages.

There are many types of B vitamins (often called the B complex) and these serve many purposes in your dog's body. They are necessary for reproduction and healthy fetal growth, normal puppy growth, healthy skin and appetite, and normal vision. The B vitamins are also needed for many chemical processes in your dog's body.

Dogs synthesize vitamin C within their body (unlike people, who do not do this). However, many experts feel that in times of stress, additional vitamin C is needed. Vitamin C is an antioxidant and is necessary for healing and growth, for a healthy immune system, and for many chemical processes within the body, including the metabolism of several minerals.

Vitamin D is needed for healthy bones, teeth, and muscles. Vitamin E is an essential vitamin for healthy organ functions. Vitamin K is needed for the normal clotting of blood, among other body processes. E and K are also antioxidants.

Minerals

Minerals are needed for many bodily processes, and in many cases, they act with vitamins or enzymes to perform their function. For example, calcium and phosphorus act together with vitamin D to help your dog grow. They also produce healthy bones, aid in muscle development, and aid in reproduction and lactation.

> **TIP**
>
> A good diet will contain all of the vitamins most dogs need. However, many owners feel that supplementation is an extra assurance of good nutrition. If you decide you would like to add a supplement, talk to your veterinarian first, as many vitamins can cause harm when given in excess.

Other essential minerals include potassium, which is needed for normal growth and healthy nerves and muscles; sodium and chlorine are necessary for a good appetite and energy; and magnesium is needed for a healthy nervous system. Iron is needed for healthy blood, and iodine prevents goiter. Copper is needed for strong bones and, like iron, is necessary for healthy blood. Zinc is involved in normal growth, assists antioxidants, and is needed for healthy skin.

Commercial Dog Foods

Commercial dog foods today are very different from those available twenty years ago. Although cheaper, plain label or generic foods are still for sale, there are far more foods of excellent quality today. These foods are balanced to provide your dog with good nutrition in a variety of formulas, from puppyhood through old age.

Dry dog foods come in a variety of shapes and sizes. Some are in meal form, with the ingredients simply mixed together. Others are shaped and baked, extruded, or pelleted. Some dry foods are primarily cereal grains with some meat, and others are primarily meat with carbohydrates mixed in.

Canned dog foods are primarily meat and water, although some will also include vegetables. Dehydrated foods are usually meat and vegetables, and frozen foods may be only meats, or meats and vegetables.

Semi-moist foods are high in salt, sugar, and preservatives. Although dogs eagerly eat these foods, they do so because of these ingredients, none of which are good for your Bichon.

Make sure you learn how to read a dog food label so that you understand exactly what you're feeding your dog.

In answer to consumers' demands for better quality foods, several dog food companies are now selling foods of different types of formulations, including frozen and dehydrated foods. The dehydrated foods are raw foods processed by dehydration. The foods must be mixed with water before serving. For owners who want to give their dog a food made from more natural ingredients that have been processed less than dry dog foods, these foods might be the answer. The frozen foods may be either raw foods processed by freezing or cooked foods that have been frozen. These foods must be thawed before serving.

Homemade Diets

Homemade diets of various kinds have grown in popularity over the last few years as owners have become more concerned about their dogs' nutrition. Many dog owners feel they can provide better quality ingredients in a diet tailored especially for their dog. Some of these diets are made from raw ingredients (such as raw meats and fresh vegetables and fruits), and others are cooked foods.

Although many of these dog owners are very enthusiastic about the results, many veterinarians are still skeptical. Formulating a complete and balanced diet

Reading Dog Food Labels

Dog food labels are not always easy to read, but if you know what to look for they can tell you a lot about what your dog is eating.

- The label should have a statement saying the dog food meets or exceeds the American Association of Feed Control Officials (AAFCO) nutritional guidelines. If the dog food doesn't meet AAFCO guidelines, it can't be considered complete and balanced, and can cause nutritional deficiencies.
- The guaranteed analysis lists the minimum percentages of crude protein and crude fat and the maximum percentages of crude fiber and water. AAFCO requires a minimum of 18 percent crude protein for adult dogs and 22 percent crude protein for puppies on a dry matter basis (that means with the water removed; canned foods should have more protein because they have more water). Dog food must also have a minimum of 5 percent crude fat for adults and 8 percent crude fat for puppies.
- The ingredients list the most common item in the food first, and so on until you get to the least common item, which is listed last.
- Look for a dog food that lists an animal protein source first, such as chicken or poultry meal, beef or beef byproducts, and that has other protein sources listed among the top five ingredients. That's because a food that lists chicken, wheat, wheat gluten, corn, and wheat fiber as the first five ingredients has more chicken than wheat, but may not have more chicken than all the grain products put together.
- Other ingredients may include a carbohydrate source, fat, vitamins and minerals, preservatives, fiber, and sometimes other additives purported to be healthy.
- Some grocery store brands may add artificial colors, sugar, and fillers—all of which should be avoided.

can be very difficult and nutritional deficiencies often do not show up until a dog is quite sick.

A sound alternative to a homemade diet might be one of the commercial raw food diets. There are several frozen raw foods available commercially, as well one excellent raw food that is dehydrated.

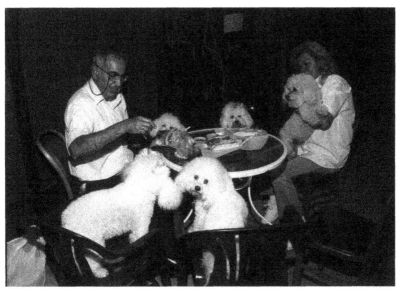

It's not easy to properly formulate a homemade diet for your dog.

Nutrition for a Lifetime

Cheap dog food is rarely cheap. It usually appears again in the form of veterinary bills. Cheaper foods are made from cheaper ingredients of lesser quality. For example, grains grown in mineral-poor soils will not nourish your dog! Chicken heads, beaks, feet, and feathers are still chicken parts, but they really shouldn't have a place in your Bichon's dog food.

When choosing the right dog food for your Bichon, choose a food that is made by a reputable company. Do some research about the food. The *Whole Dog Journal* rates dog foods according to several criteria, including the nutritional value of the ingredients. Check out the dog foods rated best and see if any are available in your area. These foods may seem expensive, but because they are nutrient-dense, you feed your dog less (and pick up less waste, too), so they end up costing almost the same as a food that seems cheaper.

If you decide to change foods, do so gradually. Add one-third of the new food to two-thirds of the old food for a week, and then increase the new food so you're feeding half and half. On the third week, change the ratio to two-thirds of the new food and one-third of the old food. By the fourth week, the dog can eat just the new food. If at any point during the change your Bichon has diarrhea,

Pet Food vs. People Food

Many of the foods we eat are excellent sources of nutrients—after all, we do just fine on them. But dogs, just like us, need the right combination of meat and other ingredients for a complete and balanced diet, and a bowl of meat doesn't provide that. In the wild, dogs eat the fur, skin, bones, and guts of their prey, and even the contents of the stomach.

This doesn't mean your dog can't eat what you eat. A little meat, dairy, bread, some fruits, or vegetables as a treat are great. Fresh foods have natural enzymes that processed foods don't have. Just remember, we're talking about the same food you eat, not the gristly, greasy leftovers you would normally toss in the trash. Stay away from sugar, too, and remember that chocolate is toxic to dogs.

If you want to share your food with your dog, be sure the total amount you give her each day doesn't make up more than 15 percent of her diet, and that the rest of what you feed her is a top-quality complete and balanced dog food. (More people food could upset the balance of nutrients in the commercial food.)

Can your dog eat an entirely homemade diet? Certainly, if you are willing to work at it. Any homemade diet will have to be carefully balanced, with all the right nutrients in just the right amounts. It requires a lot of research to make a proper homemade diet, but it can be done. It's best to work with a veterinary nutritionist.

increase the amount of the old food, decrease the new food slightly, and make the change even more gradual.

Your Bichon will grow quickly from a fuzzy handful of a puppy to a sturdy adult. Increase her food proportionately as she's growing but watch her weight. A heavy Bichon is not a happy one! As a puppy, from 7 to 20 weeks of age, your Bichon should eat three small meals a day. After 5 months of age, she can eat two meals a day, morning and evening.

Growing puppies may need to be fed more often than adults.

Do not free feed your Bichon (leave food out all day) so that she can snack as she wishes. Although this is easy for dog owners, there are several good reasons why you shouldn't do it. First of all, if your Bichon gets sick, the first thing your vet will ask is, "How is Sweetie's appetite?" and "How much did she eat today?" If your dog snacks all day and never has a real meal at set times, you won't be able to answer those questions. In addition, feeding is tied in with training. Behaviorally, the giver of the food is psychologically very important. And last but certainly not least, food left out all day can spoil, get stale, and attracts pests—including mice, rats, ants, and other vermin.

You will be able to tell that your Bichon's diet is appropriate; just watch the results. She should have plenty of energy for walks and play, should be bright eyed and alert, and her coat should be shiny and soft. Her weight should be good for her size; neither too thin nor too fat.

When There's a Problem

If your Bichon is having problems with nutrition, those problems may show up as a dull, lifeless coat that's brittle and coarse, or as a lack of energy for daily activities. Unfortunately, these may also be signs of other health problems, so a visit to the veterinarian is in order.

If you offer your dog food from the table, she'll become a beggar.

As your Bichon grows older, her nutritional needs will change. Many dogs can continue eating the same food, especially if the label says it's rated for all life stages, but she may need less food as her activity level slows. If she's having dental problems, she may need softer food. If her appetite is waning due to old age or health problems, she might be more apt to eat if her food is softened or warmed. Old dogs often do better on several small meals throughout the day rather than two larger meals.

Seven Easily Avoided Errors

We all make mistakes. Unfortunately, though, when you make a mistake with your Bichon's diet, it can have devastating results. So here are some of the most common feeding mistakes dog owners make.

1. Don't feed your Bichon chocolate, raisins, grapes, macadamia nuts, onions, or any other highly spiced, greasy, or salty foods. The first five ingredients are bad for dogs—even toxic—and the last three foods can cause gastrointestinal upset.
2. Don't believe the ads encouraging you to change your dog's diet. Dogs do not need to vary their food choices. In fact, that can lead to an upset tummy. Dogs do best when they eat on a regular schedule and eat the same well-balanced food each day.
3. If you change foods for a specific reason, feed the new food for at least six weeks. It takes several weeks for a new food to change a nutritional deficiency or solve a problem caused by food.
4. Don't fill up your Bichon with table scraps. Your Bichon has a small stomach and table scraps will fill her up quickly. If she's had table scraps, she isn't going to want to eat her dinner. Besides, if she's fed from the table, she's going to become an accomplished beggar and that's a very bad habit!
5. Don't give your Bichon any bones except raw knuckle bones. Cooked bones splinter, and chicken, turkey, and pork bones can shatter. Bichons are small but can still put forth some jaw power.

6. Don't free feed and don't leave the food bowl down for longer than ten to fifteen minutes. If your Bichon has walked away from her food bowl, she's done. Pick up her bowl. If she's left food in the bowl, she's had enough; don't feed her anything else until the next scheduled mealtime. She will learn to eat when and what she's fed.

7. Don't forget to bring food and water from home when you're traveling. In an unfamiliar area it may be tough to find your dog's food and changing foods abruptly can cause gastrointestinal upset. That can quickly spoil a trip.

Chapter 7

Grooming Your Bichon Frise

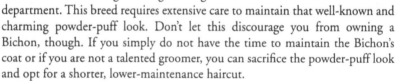

The Bichon Frise is a high-maintenance dog in the grooming department. This breed requires extensive care to maintain that well-known and charming powder-puff look. Don't let this discourage you from owning a Bichon, though. If you simply do not have the time to maintain the Bichon's coat or if you are not a talented groomer, you can sacrifice the powder-puff look and opt for a shorter, lower-maintenance haircut.

Grooming can also help cement your relationship with your dog. By handling him often, kindly and gently, and touching every part of his body as you care for him, you can teach him to trust you. He learns that you can brush and comb him, remove ticks, clean his ears and teeth, and that you will be gentle and respectful of him as you do so.

Grooming Equipment

First let's discuss what equipment you'll need to keep your Bichon neat, tidy, and free of parasites and skin problems. You will need a blow dryer with a gentle setting, a pair of metal grooming scissors, a medium-size oval wire pin brush, a small slicker brush (a brush with bent wire pins), and a metal comb. You will also need a pair of nail clippers (I like the scissors type) and styptic powder. For cleaning the ears you will need a hemostat with a blunt tip, ear powder, alcohol, and cotton balls. For cleaning teeth you will need a small, soft child's toothbrush and some baking soda.

You will also need a table where you can do this grooming. If you like to stand while you groom, you can find grooming tables at larger pet supply stores or in pet supply catalogs. If you prefer to sit, just use any table that's the right height for you. You can put a towel or a rubber-backed throw rug on the table to keep your Bichon from slipping.

The Bichon's Coat

The adult Bichon has a double coat. This means that he has an outer coat and an undercoat. The undercoat is soft and silky. At maturity, the outer coat has a harsher texture because of the guard hairs. The soft puppy coat starts getting guard hairs around the age of six months and you will notice this happening first on the lower back. During this change, your puppy will need frequent brushing so the coat does not become matted. Dematting is not only time-consuming, but it is also uncomfortable for the puppy. The easiest thing to do is prevent it.

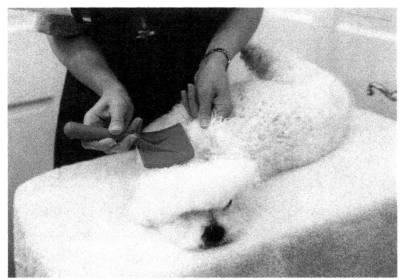

Your Bichon's double coat will need lots of brushing all over to keep it free from mats. Here, the long hair on the ears is being brushed with a slicker brush.

Brushing and Combing

The coat must always be brushed and combed through thoroughly before bathing. If mats get wet, the hair gets tighter, making dematting next to impossible.

The dog needs to be taught to lie down on his side for the brushing and drying sessions. This can best be accomplished by getting on the floor with him, patting the floor and giving him the "lie down" command. You will need to gently lift him and ease him onto his side on the floor. Once he is in the correct position, begin to gently stroke him. After several training sessions, when he's willingly lying down on his side, you can introduce him to the raised area you will use as the grooming table. Practice the "lie down" command several times and remember—*lavish him with praise.* This is a training session, not punishment time!

Once you and your Bichon have mastered this feat, you are both ready for the brushing. First, start with the slicker brush. Save the pin brush for the tail, neck, and head area, as these spots have the longest hair. With the dog on his side, use the slicker brush to brush all the way to the skin. Never brush the coat of a Bichon with long strokes, because this only fluffs the outer coat. Instead, do small sections at a time, beginning at the hips and working toward the head, brushing from the skin out toward the end of each brushful of coat.

After you have brushed the legs, tummy, sides, and chest with the slicker brush, start doing the remaining area with the pin brush. Take small sections of hair and brush all the way down to the skin.

These three guys are showing off their pet trims.

If at any time during your brushing you do hit a mat, try to break it up with your fingers. Once you have pulled it apart, hold the mat in one hand and brush it with the other. When you feel that the mat has been removed, comb out the area of the mat and make sure the entire mat is indeed removed.

After the entire body is brushed, you will need to comb through the dog's coat. Again, do not make long strokes over the top of the coat. Lift the hair so you can see a section of the dog's skin and start combing as close to the skin as possible, pulling the comb to the very ends of the coat. This is the true test of whether you have removed all mats.

After you've gotten familiar with the proper brushing and combing methods, it will only take you ten to fifteen minutes to groom your dog. The Bichon needs a thorough brushing two to three times a week; daily if he likes to play outside and gets wet or dirty.

The Pet Trim

Although a Bichon looks lovely and luxurious in his show coat, you may want to clip your dog down into what is known as a pet trim. The most popular pet trim on a Bichon is done by clipping the hair on his body close, leaving about half an inch of coat. His neck and head are left slightly longer. This "summer short" style is easy to maintain and requires fewer trips to the groomer. Plus, the shorter coat is less apt to mat.

If you opt for the longer, traditional trim, you'll need to have your dog scissored professionally every four to six weeks. Bichons can go eight to ten weeks between grooming appointments when trimmed in the shorter pet trim. Another advantage to the short cut is that you can bathe and blow-dry your dog in about twenty minutes!

Trimming Foot Pads

Although it's not mandatory that you learn to trim the hair on your Bichon's footpads, keeping this area free of hair not only helps traction but also gives you an opportunity to examine the feet and make sure the dog hasn't picked up any thorns, rocks, or other debris.

To trim the pads, lift the foot and spread the pads with one hand. Trim the hair between the pads almost flat

Trimming the hair on the foot pads helps your dog maintain his traction.

with the scissors. Never put the point of the scissors into the pad! Leave about one quarter to one half inch of hair on the bottom of the paws.

Tearing and Tear Staining

Dogs' eyes tear excessively for many reasons. Sometimes in Bichons the tear ducts may be too small, causing them to develop blockages. The ducts may also become blocked with dirt or oils on the eyelids. Allergies can cause tearing, and eyelashes that rub against the eyes can irritate the eye and cause excessive tearing.

Unfortunately, tears can stain a pretty white coat, making rust colored marks on your Bichon's face. Not only does this distract from your dog's appearance, but it signals that something is wrong in the eye (or eyes). The dampness under the eyes can also lead to problems, from irritated skin to infections.

So begin first by discussing this with your dog's veterinarian. She will need to discover why your dog is tearing and begin treatment for that. In the meantime, clean the areas on your Bichon's face several times a day with diluted baby shampoo. This is also affective for cleaning any debris or oils that might build up in the area. After washing, dry the skin and coat well. You may also want to keep the hair trimmed short under the eyes until the problem is resolved.

Bathing Your Bichon

So your Bichon needs a bath? Assuming he's in the traditional pet clip, in which the hair on his neck and head are longer than the coat on his body, you will start by holding his muzzle upward and wetting his head, exercising great care not to get water down his throat or nose. The Bichon's coat is like a thirsty sponge and it takes time to get it good and wet.

After wetting the dog thoroughly, apply a shampoo recommended for white dogs. Gently squish the shampoo into the coat. Do not scrub! Scrubbing will cause matting.

After sudsing, be sure to rinse thoroughly, as shampoo residue will cause dry skin and itching or even skin sores. When you rinse, make sure you get under each front leg (between the leg and the chest) and the groin area.

After rinsing, squeeze excess water from the dog and wrap him in a thick towel. Remove him from the tub, place him onto a clean, dry towel and begin to blot and squeeze him dry. After squeezing him dry, discard the wet towel and partially wrap him in a dry towel, exposing his only head.

Just when you think you have rinsed out all the shampoo, rinse again. Note the nonskid mat in this sink.

Blow Drying

Now you will need to blow dry your Bichon's coat. With your dryer on the low to medium setting (never high or hot!), begin to blow dry your Bichon's head. Lift a tuft of hair with the pin brush and blow it dry with quick strokes of the dryer. From the head continue down the neck and entire back. Remember—no long strokes over the top of the coat. Take a small section of hair and continue brushing and drying until there are no crinkles. Remove any wet towels and continue to blow-dry the rest of the dog's body.

If your dog has a thick, hardy coat, you may dry him with the slicker brush and switch to the pin brush for the head, neck, and tail. If his coat is brittle or silky, you should use the pin brush on the entire dog. While blow-drying, do not skip around; finish drying the entire head before continuing to the neck and beyond.

When your Bichon is dry, you will need to comb his entire coat. During this final combing, you will fluff him, for this is how the powder-puff look is achieved. When combing each section of hair, pull the comb off the body. This makes the coat stand off the body.

Towel dry your dog before you get out the blow dryer.

Now review your result. Does he look curly? If so, you did not dry each section of hair thoroughly or you dried the section without enough brushing. Brushing while drying straightens the coat.

Never bathe a coated Bichon and let him dry naturally, and never crate-dry a Bichon. (Crate-drying means a dog is contained in a wire crate with a dryer hooked to it.) If you do not blow dry the Bichon, his coat will dry kinky, resulting in an unkempt look and a tendency to mat.

A Handy Shortcut

Don't have the time to bathe your dog and company is coming? Unless he is wet or muddy, he can be spruced up in five to ten minutes and look just fine. Shake baby powder into his coat and pat it in. Then brush the powder into the coat. Voila! Whiter, fresher, and very poofy!

Make sure you powder him outside the house or in your tub so the powder doesn't get everywhere. Make sure, too, that you use baby powder. Don't use perfumed talcum powders, as many of these contain ingredients that could be dangerous to your dog.

Cleaning Ears

Bichons grow long hairs inside their ears and those hairs need to be removed, because they attract dirt and keep the ears too damp, which can lead to ear infections. You or your dog's groomer must remove this hair. Although the process is initially tough for some owners, you can learn how to do it.

While the dog is lying on his side, shake some ear powder (or baby powder) into the ear canal. This coats the hair so it can be removed with ease. Once the hair is coated, begin pulling it out gently with the hemostat. Take small amounts at a time so as not to hurt the dog. If done properly once a month, this will not be an unpleasant experience.

After all hair has been removed from the ear canal area, it is time to clean the ear. Apply a liquid ear cleaner to a cotton ball and squeeze out the excess. Use the cotton ball to wipe out the entire ear. If there is a reddish-brown color on the cotton ball accompanied by an odor, the dog probably has an ear infection and needs to see his veterinarian.

Trimming Toenails

Nails need to be trimmed a couple of times a month, depending on how much your dog naturally wears them down. Your Bichon's nails should not make a clicking sound when he walks across a hard floor. Before trimming your dog's nails, make sure your nail clippers have a nice, sharp edge and that styptic powder is nearby.

Start by lifting the dog's foot so you can see his nails in profile. If the nail is clear or light in color, you will be able to see the quick—the bundle of blood vessels and nerves running down the center. Cut the nail just beyond the quick. If you cut too deeply, the nail will start to bleed. If this happens, coat the end of the bleeding nail with styptic powder (cornstarch will also do in a pinch) until

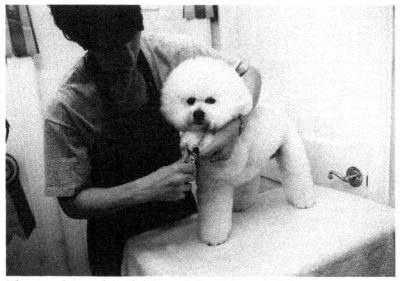

When you can hear your dog's nails clicking on the floor, it's time to trim them.

the bleeding stops. If the nail is black and you cannot see the quick, clip only the tip of the hooked part of the nail, or, if you're brave, trim it to the same length as the clear nails on the same paw.

Take care not to squeeze the dog's paws too tightly when trimming nails, for this will cause discomfort that he'll associate with nail trimming.

Do not forget to cut your dog's dewclaws if he has them. Dewclaws are located on the inside front and rear leg, near the dog's wrist area. Most breeders have dewclaws removed when the pups are a few days old. It's acceptable to some breeders to leave front dewclaws intact, but rear dewclaws on the Bichon are never acceptable.

Cleaning Teeth

Your Bichon will need to have his teeth brushed two or three times a week. Using a child's soft toothbrush dipped into a paste of water and baking soda, start brushing gently. If your Bichon has healthy gums, they will be firm and pinkish in color. If they bleed and are red and swollen, he has a dental problem and needs to see his veterinarian.

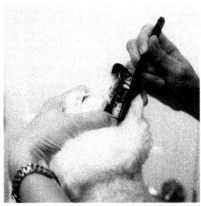

Brushing your dog's teeth regularly will prevent a great many problems.

If your dog fights the toothbrush, use a piece of gauze wrapped around your finger and dipped into the paste. Gently rub the gauze against the teeth and base of the gums.

You don't have to do the dog's entire mouth in one sitting, especially if your Bichon isn't used to this yet. Instead, clean one quarter of his mouth, praise him, and make a big fuss over him. The next day do another quarter of his mouth, and so on. Your dog learns to associate this process with lots of praise and petting from you, and you aren't making him put up with it for too long.

New Products in the Fight Against Fleas

At one time, battling fleas meant exposing your dog and yourself to toxic dips, sprays, powders, and collars. But today there are flea preventives that work very well and are safe for your dog, you, and the environment. The two most common types are insect growth regulators (IGRs), which stop the immature flea from developing or maturing, and adult flea killers. To deal with an active infestation, experts usually recommend a product that has both.

These next-generation flea fighters generally come in one of two forms:

- **Topical treatments or spot-ons.** These products are applied to the skin, usually between the shoulder blades. The product is absorbed through the skin into the dog's system. Among the most widely available spot-ons are Advantage (kills adult fleas and larvae), Revolution (kills adult fleas), Frontline Plus (kills adult fleas and larvae, plus an IGR), K-9 Advantix (kills adult fleas and larvae), and BioSpot (kills adult fleas and larvae, plus an IGR).
- **Systemic products.** This is a pill your dog swallows that transmits a chemical throughout the dog's bloodstream. When a flea bites the dog, it picks up this chemical, which then prevents the flea's eggs from developing. Among the most widely available systemic products are Program (kills larvae only, plus an IGR) and Capstar (kills adult fleas).

Make sure you read all the labels and apply the products exactly as recommended, and that you check to make sure they are safe for puppies.

Making Your Environment Flea Free

If there are fleas on your dog, there are fleas in your home, yard, and car, even if you can't see them. Take these steps to combat them.

In your home:

- Wash whatever is washable (the dog bed, sheets, blankets, pillow covers, slipcovers, curtains, etc.).
- Vacuum everything else in your home—furniture, floors, rugs, everything. Pay special attention to the folds and crevices in upholstery, cracks between floorboards, and the spaces between the floor and the baseboards. Flea larvae are sensitive to sunlight, so inside the house they prefer deep carpet, bedding, and cracks and crevices.
- When you're done, throw the vacuum cleaner bag away—in an outside garbage can.
- Use a nontoxic flea-killing powder, such as Flea Busters or Zodiac FleaTrol, to treat your carpets (but remember, it does not control fleas elsewhere in the house). The powder stays deep in the carpet and kills fleas (using a form of boric acid) for up to a year.
- If you have a particularly serious flea problem, consider using a fogger or long-lasting spray to kill any adult and larval fleas, or having a professional exterminator treat your home.

External Parasites

When you brush and comb your dog, it's a good idea to look closely for any lumps or bumps and signs of external parasites. External parasites include fleas, ticks, and mites. All are looking for a good home, and your Bichon could be just perfect as far as they're concerned!

Fleas are pesky little bugs that bite your dog for a drop of blood, which the flea then ingests. Fleas live in the environment (your house and the yard) and just jump on your dog for a meal. Fleas can cause skin irritations and allergies, and can transmit diseases and parasites. There are many new flea control products that are much safer than the old ones, so talk to your veterinarian and groomer for information regarding flea control.

Ticks come in a variety of sizes, from pinhead to almost the size of a dime, and can be dark brown, medium brown, or even gray. Ticks bury their head in

In your car:

- Take out the floor mats and hose them down with a strong stream of water, then hang them up to dry in the sun.
- Wash any towels, blankets, or other bedding you regularly keep in the car.
- Thoroughly vacuum the entire interior of your car, paying special attention to the seams between the bottom and back of the seats.
- When you're done, throw the vacuum cleaner bag away—in an outside garbage can.

In your yard:

- Flea larvae prefer shaded areas that have plenty of organic material and moisture, so rake the yard thoroughly and bag all the debris in tightly sealed bags.
- Spray your yard with an insecticide that has residual activity for at least thirty days. Insecticides that use a form of boric acid are nontoxic. Some newer products contain an insect growth regulator (such as fenoxycarb) and need to be applied only once or twice a year.
- For an especially difficult flea problem, consider having an exterminator treat your yard.
- Keep your yard free of piles of leaves, weeds, and other organic debris. Be especially careful in shady, moist areas, such as under bushes.

the dog's skin to drink blood, and when they do, they can become engorged. While eating, they use their saliva to keep the dog's blood flowing. The saliva can pass along diseases to the dog, from Lyme disease to Rocky Mountain spotted fever. Many of the new flea products also work on ticks, but if you find a tick on your dog, remove it carefully.

Sarcoptic mange is caused by mites. A Bichon with mange will scratch and develop red, crusty areas on his skin. This needs to be treated by a veterinarian right away.

Demodex or follicular mange is caused by a different kind of mites. This type of mange is usually not as itchy as sarcoptic mange. It also needs veterinary treatment right away.

External parasites of any kind should be treated immediately and should never be ignored. Their potential to cause your dog distress, discomfort, and harm are too great.

How to Get Rid of a Tick

Although Frontline, K-9 Advantix, and BioSpot, the new generation of flea fighters, are partially effective in killing ticks once they are on your dog, they are not 100 percent effective and will not keep ticks from biting your dog in the first place. During tick season (which, depending on where you live, can be spring, summer, and/or fall), examine your dog every day for ticks. Pay particular attention to your dog's neck, behind the ears, the armpits, and the groin.

When you find a tick, use a pair of tweezers to grasp the tick as close as possible to the dog's skin and pull it out using firm, steady pressure. Check to make sure you get the whole tick (mouth parts left in your dog's skin can cause an infection), then dab the wound with a little hydrogen peroxide and some antibiotic ointment. Watch for signs of inflammation.

Ticks carry very serious diseases that are transmittable to humans, so dispose of the tick safely. Never crush it between your fingers. Don't flush it down the toilet either, because the tick will survive the trip and infect another animal. Instead, use the tweezers to place the tick in a tight-sealing jar or plastic dish with a little alcohol, put on the lid and dispose of the container in an outdoor garbage can. Wash the tweezers thoroughly with hot water and alcohol.

Chapter 8

Keeping Your Bichon Frise Healthy

Bichons are, for the most part, active, strong, sturdy, healthy small dogs. They are alert and inquisitive, and love to play. They can easily live to 14 years of age, and dogs living to 16 are not unusual. There are a few health problems that can harm your Bichon, however, and it's important that you recognize them if they appear. After all, your Bichon cannot care for herself; she relies on you for her continued good health.

Choosing a Vet

Your dog's veterinarian should be someone who makes you feel as if your Bichon's health is as much a priority for him as it is for you. Choose a clinic that is immaculate and in which the staff appears to be well-trained and helpful. You can find a good vet by asking for referrals from other dog owners, including friends and neighbors. If your puppy was purchased locally, ask the breeder for a reference.

When you have the names of a couple of veterinarians, call and make an appointment with each of them. Be prepared to pay for an office visit, since you will be taking up some of the vet's time. Ask the vet whether he's familiar with Bichons and if he is, does he enjoy working with them? Just as anyone else may have favorite dog breeds, so do vets. Some also like big dogs more than small dogs. You want a vet who likes Bichons and enjoys working with them.

After you, your veterinarian will be the most important person in your dog's life.

Ask the vet about his office procedures, hours, emergency policies, and after-hours arrangements. If a dog spends the night, is there anyone in the clinic with the dog or is she alone? When your questions have been answered and you feel very comfortable with this vet, make another appointment and this time bring in your Bichon. You want the vet to see her when she's healthy so that she can be examined, weighed, and vitals taken (pulse, temperature, and respiration). You may also want to do some baseline blood work so that if there is a problem in the future, your vet will know what is normal for your dog.

Preventive Care

There are some easy steps you can take to help make sure your Bichon stays in good health throughout her life. As well as saving your pet infinite discomfort, these preventive steps will save you money and heartache in the long run.

When you are snuggling or grooming your Bichon, take a few minutes to run your hands over her. Feel for any bumps, sores, or anything out of the ordinary. Be attentive to how much she eats and drinks and the way she moves when she exercises. You want to recognize what is normal for your dog so that anything out of the ordinary stands out. Changes may signal that something's wrong, and early detection can save lots of trouble.

Why Spay and Neuter?

Breeding dogs is a serious undertaking that should only be part of a well-planned breeding program. Why? Because dogs pass on their physical and behavioral problems to their offspring. Even healthy, well-behaved dogs can pass on problems in their genes.

Is your dog so sweet that you'd like to have a litter of puppies just like her? If you breed her to another dog, the pups will not have the same genetic heritage she has. Breeding her *parents* again will increase the odds of a similar pup, but even then, the puppies in the second litter could inherit different genes. In fact, *there is no way to breed a dog to be just like another dog.*

Meanwhile, thousands and thousands of dogs are killed in animal shelters every year simply because they have no homes. Casual breeding is a big contributor to this problem.

If you don't plan to breed your dog, is it still a good idea to spay her or neuter him? Yes!

When you spay your female:

- You avoid her heat cycles, during which she discharges blood and scent.
- It greatly reduces the risk of mammary cancer and eliminates the risk of pyometra (an often fatal infection of the uterus) and uterine cancer.
- It prevents unwanted pregnancies.
- It reduces dominance behaviors and aggression.

When you neuter your male:

- It curbs the desire to roam and to fight with other males.
- It greatly reduces the risk of prostate cancer and eliminates the risk of testicular cancer.
- It helps reduce leg lifting and mounting behavior.
- It reduces dominance behaviors and aggression.

Vaccines

What vaccines dogs need and how often they need them has been a subject of controversy for several years. Researchers, health care professionals, vaccine manufacturers, and dog owners do not always agree on which vaccines each dog needs or how often booster shots must be given.

In 2003, the American Animal Hospital Association released vaccination guidelines and recommendations that have helped dog owners and veterinarians sort through much of the controversy and conflicting information. The guidelines designate four vaccines as core, or essential, because of the serious nature of the diseases and their widespread distribution. These are canine distemper virus, canine parvovirus, canine adenovirus-2, and rabies. The general recommendations for their use (except rabies, for which you must follow local laws) are:

- Vaccinate puppies at 6–8 weeks, 9–11 weeks, and 12–14 weeks.
- Give a booster shot when the dog is 1 year old.
- Give a subsequent booster shot every three years, unless there are risk factors that make it necessary to vaccinate more or less often.

An important part of preventive healthcare involves spaying your female or neutering your male Bichon. The health benefits are explained in the box on page 79.

Vital Vaccinations

Your Bichon's breeder or rescue group volunteer will have given you a list of the vaccinations your dog had. Make sure you bring this list with you to the first appointment your Bichon has with the veterinarian. If you forget this list, he may recommend duplicate vaccinations and you don't want to do that.

Noncore vaccines should only be considered for those dogs who risk exposure to a particular disease because of geographic area, lifestyle, frequency of travel, or other issues. They include vaccines against distemper-measles virus, canine parainfluenza virus, leptospirosis, Bordetella bronchiseptica, and Borrelia burgdorferi (Lyme disease).

Vaccines that are not generally recommended because the disease poses little risk to dogs or is easily treatable, or the vaccine has not been proven to be effective, are those against Giardia, canine coronavirus, and canine adenovirus-1.

Often, combination injections are given to puppies, with one shot containing several core and noncore vaccines. Your veterinarian may be reluctant to use separate shots that do not include the noncore vaccines, because they must be specially ordered. If you are concerned about these noncore vaccines, talk to your vet.

These vaccinations, both the ones the breeder gave the puppy and the ones your vet will recommend, are the best way to prevent a variety of diseases. The number and type of vaccines depend on where you live. If you plan on traveling with your Bichon, make sure you tell your vet, as he may recommend other vaccines.

Internal Parasites

Your veterinarian will want to check your Bichon for internal parasites, and don't be offended by this. Although many Bichon owners say, "My Bichon cannot have worms!" actually she can! No matter how carefully you care for your Bichon, she could still become infested by worms or other internal parasites.

Worms can be passed from a mother dog to her pups.

Your vet can check for roundworms, whipworms, hookworms, and tapeworms by examining a fresh a stool sample. If the sample turns up positive, your vet will recommend medication and will probably ask that you bring in another stool sample in a few weeks to make sure the infestation is cleared up.

Heartworms are also an internal parasite, but instead of living in the digestive tract as other worms do, this parasite infests the blood (in its early stages) and then, as an adult, infests the heart. Your vet will need a blood sample to check for heartworm and, if that shows up negative, he will recommend a preventive so your dog will not become infested. Treatment for dogs who test positive for heartworms is very difficult and dangerous, so prevention is definitely the best option.

Common Health Problems

Your Bichon Frise may never face any of the following health problems, but you should be aware of them so you can recognize them and get her the proper treatment.

Anal Glands

If your Bichon is dragging her rear end along the floor, her anal glands are probably blocked and could potentially be infected. The anal glands are located along each side of the anus and secrete a small amount of a smelly, oily fluid with each bowel movement. When blocked, the glands can become swollen, painful, and infected.

Take your Bichon to the veterinarian's office, where the glands can be checked, expressed, and medicated if necessary. The vet will also show you what to look for in case of future problems.

Luxating Patella

If you see your Bichon hop and skip with one or both back legs, especially when running, she may have luxating patella, or slipping kneecaps. This can happen in one or both rear legs. Although the patella can be injured during rough play or exercise, most patella problems are structural and, therefore, genetic in nature. When the dog moves, the patella slips from its correct position. This causes pain, pinching, or a restriction of movement for that leg. Although the dog can learn to handle minor cases (stretching the leg to move the patella back into position), sometimes surgery is needed to correct the problem.

A healthy dog should be able to run and jump without problems or pain.

Allergies

Allergies can occur in any dog of any breed, and the Bichon Frise is no exception. The most common causes of allergies include tree and grass pollens and some foods, including wheat, corn, and rice. Licking and chewing, often to the point where the skin is red and inflamed, are common symptoms.

Talk to your veterinarian about your dog's allergies. If he recommends allergy tests, do consider it. Although the tests are expensive, you can then find out exactly what your dog is allergic to and can help your dog avoid it.

Handling Common Problems

Vomiting

If your Bichon has no other symptoms if illness but vomits once or twice (especially if she throws up grass), just keep an eye on her. She may have simply eaten something that doesn't agree with her. However, if your Bichon continues to throw up, has dry heaves, or also has diarrhea, call your veterinarian.

Diarrhea

At the first sign of diarrhea, remove all food for twenty-four hours except in the case of the very old or very young—for those dogs, call a vet right away. If your Bichon's stools are better after twenty-four hours, feed her a small meal of boiled rice and chicken, and gradually (over three days) wean her back onto her normal food.

If the diarrhea is severe or is bloody, call your veterinarian right away. Also call if your Bichon appears to be straining to pass something and cannot, or if the stool has a particularly bad odor.

Limping

If your Bichon is limping for no apparent reason (check her paws for cuts or fox-tails or burrs) and has no other symptoms, just watch for twenty-four hours and see if she's better. She may have twisted or pulled something and is just sore. If she's still limping the next day, call your vet.

Coughing

Coughing can be a sign of many different problems, from kennel cough to heart disease. An occasional cough is usually nothing to be worried about, but repeated coughing needs to be checked out by your vet.

Emergency How-To's

Muzzling

Even the sweetest Bichon may bite when she is in pain or frightened. Using a muzzle protects you from your dog in these situations. Use a piece of soft material, such as the leg of a pair of pantyhose, and wrap the material twice around

Dogs can fade quickly in the heat. Limit your dog's exercise on hot days.

your Bichon's muzzle. Bring the ends behind your Bichon's head and tie them in the back. Leave the muzzle on until your Bichon has been treated or seen by the vet.

Serious Injuries

The Bichon's small size makes her much easier to immobilize and transport than larger dogs. If you suspect she's been hit by a car, broken a bone, or has severely hurt herself in another way, you want to immediately immobilize her. Take a piece of board (such as a piece of bookshelf) or the top of a TV tray. Moving her as little as possible, lift her onto this board. Using soft material (scarves, bathrobe ties, or pantyhose), tie her to this board so she cannot move. Get her to the vet as soon as possible.

Heat Exhaustion and Heatstroke

Heat exhaustion and heatstroke can be life-threatening problems. If your Bichon has gotten overheated by too much exercise on a hot day or by being out in the heat too long, she will pant excessively with heaving breathing. Her saliva will be thick and her tongue may be very red. She may be unsteady on her feet and may even fall. She may refuse to drink.

When to Call the Veterinarian

Go to the vet right away or take your dog to an emergency veterinary clinic if:

- Your dog is choking
- Your dog is having trouble breathing
- Your dog has been injured and you cannot stop the bleeding within a few minutes
- Your dog has been stung or bitten by an insect and the site is swelling
- Your dog has been bitten by a snake
- Your dog has been bitten by another animal (including a dog) and shows any swelling or bleeding
- Your dog has touched, licked, or in any way been exposed to a poison
- Your dog has been burned by either heat or caustic chemicals
- Your dog has been hit by a car
- Your dog has any obvious broken bones or cannot put any weight on one of her limbs
- Your dog has a seizure

Make an appointment to see the vet as soon as possible if:

- Your dog has been bitten by a cat, another dog, or a wild animal
- Your dog has been injured and is still limping an hour later

She needs to get to the vet's office right away, but you need to begin cooling her down as you do so. Wet her down with cool but not cold water, and run cool water through her mouth even if she doesn't want to drink. If your car has air conditioning, turn that on as you take her to the vet's office. Call them to let them know an emergency is on the way.

Snakebite

Symptoms following a snakebite include swelling, labored breathing, glazed eyes, and drooling. The best first aid you can give your dog is to keep her warm

- Your dog has unexplained swelling or redness
- Your dog's appetite changes
- Your dog vomits repeatedly and can't seem to keep food down, or drools excessively while eating
- You see any changes in your dog's urination or defecation (pain during elimination, change in regular habits, blood in urine or stool, diarrhea, foul-smelling stool)
- Your dog scoots her rear end on the floor
- Your dog's energy level, attitude, or behavior changes for no apparent reason
- Your dog has crusty or cloudy eyes, or excessive tearing or discharge
- Your dog's nose is dry or chapped, hot, crusty, or runny
- Your dog's ears smell foul, have a dark discharge, or seem excessively waxy
- Your dog's gums are inflamed or bleeding, her teeth look brown, or her breath is foul
- Your dog's skin is red, flaky, itchy, or inflamed, or she keeps chewing at certain spots
- Your dog's coat is dull, dry, brittle, or bare in spots
- Your dog's paws are red, swollen, tender, cracked, or the nails are split or too long
- Your dog is panting excessively, wheezing, unable to catch her breath, breathing heavily or sounds strange when she breathes

and still as you get her to the vet's office right away. Call them and let them know a snakebite case is on the way. Make sure you can describe the snake to them.

Bleeding

If your Bichon is bleeding, it's important to keep calm. If you're upset, your Bichon will get even more upset and will then bleed even more. So control yourself first.

How to Make a Canine First-Aid Kit

If your dog hurts herself, even a minor cut, it can be very upsetting for both of you. Having a first-aid kit handy will help you to help her, calmly and efficiently. What should be in your canine first-aid kit?

- Antibiotic ointment
- Antiseptic and antibacterial cleansing wipes
- Benadryl
- Cotton-tipped applicators
- Disposable razor
- Elastic wrap bandages
- Extra leash and collar
- First-aid tape of various widths
- Gauze bandage roll
- Gauze pads of different sizes, including eye pads
- Hydrogen peroxide
- Instant cold compress
- Kaopectate tablets or liquid
- Latex gloves
- Lubricating jelly
- Muzzle
- Nail clippers
- Pen, pencil, and paper for notes and directions
- Pepto-Bismol
- Round-ended scissors and pointy scissors
- Safety pins
- Sterile saline eyewash
- Thermometer (rectal)
- Tweezers

Using a clean cloth, a wad of paper towels, or even your hand, apply pressure to the wound. After fifteen seconds, check to see if the bleeding has slowed. If it's still bleeding, reapply pressure. When the bleeding slows, apply a bandage to the wound with a thick wad of gauze and get your Bichon to the vet's office.

In an emergency, your dog relies on you to know what to do.

If the wound continues to bleed heavily, or if it's spurting from an injured blood vessel, apply a pressure bandage and get your dog to the nearest veterinarian right away. If in doubt, call the veterinarian and ask for advice on what to do while you're on the way. Do not try to apply a tourniquet unless the vet advises you to do so.

The Aging Bichon

Luckily, Bichons are a long-lived breed, often reaching 14 to 16 years of age. But time can fly by way too quickly and it's hard to see a treasured friend suffer from the indignities of old age. Like us, dogs' bodies deteriorate as they age.

Cataracts are not unusual and can impair the dog's sight if they become quite opaque. They can be removed, however, if the dog is otherwise in good health.

ASPCA Animal Poison Control Center

The ASPCA Animal Poison Control Center has a staff of licensed veterinarians and board-certified toxicologists available 24 hours a day, 365 days a year. The number to call is (888) 426-4435. You will be charged a consultation fee of $50 per case, charged to most major credit cards. There is no charge for follow-up calls in critical cases. At your request, they will also contact your veterinarian. Specific treatment and information can be provided via fax. Put the number in large, legible print with your other emergency telephone numbers. Be prepared to give your name, address, and phone number; what your dog has gotten into (the amount and how long ago); your dog's breed, age, sex, and weight; and what signs and symptoms the dog is showing. You can log onto www.aspca.org and click on "Animal Poison Control Center" for more information, including a list of toxic and nontoxic plants.

Many Bichons also lose their hearing as they age, sometimes partially but other times totally. Although this can make living with the dog a challenge, many deaf dogs live out their lives quite happily.

Senility can occur in older Bichons, with the dog seeming to forget where she is, who she's with, and what she should do. New drugs can sometimes help these dogs regain some of what they've lost, at least for a while.

Bichons can also develop lumps and bumps on the skin, bladder stones, and tooth and gum disease. These problems can be simply irritating or devastating, depending upon their severity, the age of the dog, and the dog's overall health. It's important to have a good working relationship with your veterinarian. You need to be able to talk with him, ask questions, and express your opinions or desires. He is your partner in your Bichon's ongoing good health.

Some dogs enjoy the companionship of a youngster as they age. But not all will welcome a puppy.

At some point, though, you may need to make the decision to let your dog go. When your dog is suffering and when she is no longer enjoying life, then it may be time to give her the ultimate kindness. Again, talk to your veterinarian, preferably before it's time, so you know what the policies and procedures are. In any case, do not let your treasured Bichon suffer.

Part III

Enjoying Your Bichon Frise

Chapter 9

Training Your Bichon Frise

by Peggy Moran

Training makes your best friend better! A properly trained dog has a happier life and a longer life expectancy. He is also more appreciated by the people he encounters each day, both at home and out and about.

A trained dog walks nicely and joins his family often, going places untrained dogs cannot go. He is never rude or unruly, and he always happily comes when called. When he meets people for the first time, he greets them by sitting and waiting to be petted, rather than jumping up. At home he doesn't compete with his human family, and alone he is not destructive or overly anxious. He isn't continually nagged with words like "no," since he has learned not to misbehave in the first place. He is never shamed, harshly punished, or treated unkindly, and he is a well-loved, involved member of the family.

Sounds good, doesn't it? If you are willing to invest some time, thought, and patience, the words above could soon be used to describe your dog (though perhaps changing "he" to "she"). Educating your pet in a positive way is fun and easy, and there is no better gift you can give your pet than the guarantee of improved understanding and a great relationship.

This chapter will explain how to offer kind leadership, reshape your pet's behavior in a positive and practical way, and even get a head start on simple obedience training.

Understanding Builds the Bond

Dog training is a learning adventure on both ends of the leash. Before attempting to teach their dog new behaviors or change unwanted ones, thoughtful dog owners take the time to understand why their pets behave the way they do, and how their own behavior can be either a positive or negative influence on their dog.

Canine Nature

Loving dogs as much as we do, it's easy to forget they are a completely different species. Despite sharing our homes and living as appreciated members of our families, dogs do not think or learn exactly the same way people do. Even if you love your dog like a child, you must remember to respect the fact that he is actually a dog.

Dogs have no idea when their behavior is inappropriate from a human perspective. They are not aware of the value of possessions they chew or of messes they make or the worry they sometimes seem to cause. While people tend to look at behavior as good and bad or right and wrong, dogs just discover what works and what doesn't work. Then they behave accordingly, learning from their own experiences and increasing or reducing behaviors to improve results for themselves.

You might wonder, "But don't dogs want to please us?" My answer is yes, provided your pleasure reflects back to them in positive ways they can feel and appreciate. Dogs do things for *dog* reasons, and everything they do works for them in some way or they wouldn't be doing it!

The Social Dog

Our pets descended from animals who lived in tightly knit, cooperative social groups. Though far removed in appearance and lifestyle from their ancestors, our dogs still relate in many of the same ways their wild relatives did. And in their relationships with one another, wild canids either lead or follow.

Canine ranking relationships are not about cruelty and power; they are about achievement and abilities. Competent dogs with high levels of drive and confidence step up, while deferring dogs step aside. But followers don't get the short end of the stick; they benefit from the security of having a more competent dog at the helm.

Our domestic dogs still measure themselves against other members of their group—us! Dog owners whose actions lead to positive results have willing, secure followers. But dogs may step up and fill the void or cut loose and do their own thing when their people fail to show capable leadership. When dogs are pushy, aggressive, and rude, or independent and unwilling, it's not because they have designs on the role of "master." It is more likely their owners failed to provide consistent leadership.

Dogs in training benefit from their handler's good leadership. Their education flows smoothly because they are impressed. Being in charge doesn't require you to physically dominate or punish your dog. You simply need to make some subtle changes in the way you relate to him every day.

Lead Your Pack!

Create schedules and structure daily activities. Dogs are creatures of habit and routines will create security. Feed meals at the same times each day and also try to schedule regular walks, training practices, and toilet outings. Your predictability will help your dog be patient.

Ask your dog to perform a task. Before releasing him to food or freedom, have him do something as simple as sit on command. Teach him that cooperation earns great results!

Give a release prompt (such as "let's go") when going through doors leading outside. This is a better idea than allowing your impatient pup to rush past you.

Pet your dog when he is calm, not when he is excited. Turn your touch into a tool that relaxes and settles.

Reward desirable rather than inappropriate behavior. Petting a jumping dog (who hasn't been invited up) reinforces jumping. Pet sitting dogs, and only invite lap dogs up after they've first "asked" by waiting for your invitation.

Replace personal punishment with positive reinforcement. Show a dog what *to do,* and motivate him to want to do it, and there will be no need to punish him for what he should *not do.* Dogs naturally follow, without the need for force or harshness.

Play creatively and appropriately. Your dog will learn the most about his social rank when he is playing with you. During play, dogs work to control toys and try to get the best of one another in a friendly way. The wrong sorts of play can create problems: For example, tug of war can lead to aggressiveness. Allowing your dog to control toys during play may result in possessive guarding when he has something he really values, such as a bone. Dogs who are chased during play may later run away from you when you approach to leash them. The right kinds of play will help increase your dog's social confidence while you gently assert your leadership.

How Dogs Learn (and How They Don't)

Dog training begins as a meeting of minds—yours and your dog's. Though the end goal may be to get your dog's body to behave in a specific way, training starts as a mind game. Your dog is learning all the time by observing the consequences of his actions and social interactions. He is always seeking out what he perceives as desirable and trying to avoid what he perceives as undesirable.

He will naturally repeat a behavior that either brings him more good stuff or makes bad stuff go away (these are both types of reinforcement). He will naturally avoid a behavior that brings him more bad stuff or makes the good stuff go away (these are both types of punishment).

Both reinforcement and punishment can be perceived as either the direct result of something the dog did himself, or as coming from an outside source.

Using Life's Rewards

Your best friend is smart and he is also cooperative. When the best things in life can only be had by working with you, your dog will view you as a facilitator. You unlock doors to all of the positively reinforcing experiences he values: his freedom, his friends at the park, food, affection, walks, and play. The trained dog accompanies you through those doors and waits to see what working with you will bring.

Rewarding your dog for good behavior is called positive reinforcement, and, as we've just seen, it increases the likelihood that he will repeat that behavior. The perfect reward is anything your dog wants that is safe and appropriate. Don't limit yourself to toys, treats, and things that come directly from you. Harness life's positives—barking at squirrels, chasing a falling leaf, bounding away from you at the dog park, pausing for a moment to sniff everything—and allow your dog to earn access to those things as rewards that come from cooperating with you. When he looks at you, when he sits, when he comes when you call—any prompted behavior can earn one of life's rewards. When he works with you, he earns the things he most appreciates; but when he tries to get those things on his own, he cannot. Rather than seeing you as someone who always says "no," your dog will view you as the one who says "let's go!" He will *want* to follow.

What About Punishment?

Not only is it unnecessary to personally punish dogs, it is abusive. No matter how convinced you are that your dog "knows right from wrong," in reality he will associate personal punishment with the punisher. The resulting cowering, "guilty"-looking postures are actually displays of submission and fear. Later,

Purely Positive Reinforcement

With positive training, we emphasize teaching dogs what they should do to earn reinforcements, rather than punishing them for unwanted behaviors.

- Focus on teaching "do" rather than "don't." For example, a sitting dog isn't jumping.
- Use positive reinforcers that are valuable to your dog and the situation: A tired dog values rest; a confined dog values freedom.
- Play (appropriately)!
- Be a consistent leader.
- Set your dog up for success by anticipating and preventing problems.
- Notice and reward desirable behavior, and give him lots of attention when he is being good.
- Train ethically. Use humane methods and equipment that do not frighten or hurt your dog.
- When you are angry, walk away and plan a positive strategy.
- Keep practice sessions short and sweet. Five to ten minutes, three to five times a day is best.

when the punisher isn't around and the coast is clear, the same behavior he was punished for—such as raiding a trash can—might bring a self-delivered, very tasty result. The punished dog hasn't learned not to misbehave; he has learned to not get caught.

Does punishment ever have a place in dog training? Many people will heartily insist it does not. But dog owners often get frustrated as they try to stick to the path of all-positive reinforcement. It sure sounds great, but is it realistic, or even natural, to *never* say "no" to your dog?

A wild dog's life is not *all* positive. Hunger and thirst are both examples of negative reinforcement; the resulting discomfort motivates the wild dog to seek food and water. He encounters natural aversives such as pesky insects; mats in his coat; cold days; rainy days; sweltering hot days; and occasional run-ins with thorns, brambles, skunks, bees, and other nastiness. These all affect his behavior, as he tries to avoid the bad stuff whenever possible. The wild dog also occasionally encounters social punishers from others in his group when he gets too pushy. Starting with a growl or a snap from Mom, and later some mild and ritualized discipline from other members of his four-legged family, he learns to modify behaviors that elicit grouchy responses.

Our pet dogs don't naturally experience all positive results either, because they learn from their surroundings and from social experiences with other dogs. Watch a group of pet dogs playing together and you'll see a very old educational system still being used. As they wrestle and attempt to assert themselves, you'll notice many mouth-on-neck moments. Their playful biting is inhibited, with no intention to cause harm, but their message is clear: "Say uncle or this could hurt more!"

Observing that punishment does occur in nature, some people may feel compelled to try to be like the big wolf with their pet dogs. Becoming aggressive or heavy-handed with your pet will backfire! Your dog will not be impressed, nor will he want to follow you. Punishment causes dogs to change their behavior to avoid or escape discomfort and threats. Threatened dogs will either become very passive and offer submissive, appeasing postures, attempt to flee, or rise to the occasion and fight back. When people personally punish their dogs in an angry manner, one of these three defensive mechanisms will be triggered. Which one depends on a dog's genetic temperament as well as his past social experiences. Since we don't want to make our pets feel the need to avoid or escape us, personal punishment has no place in our training.

Remote Consequences

Sometimes, however, all-positive reinforcement is just not enough. That's because not all reinforcement comes from us. An inappropriate behavior can be self-reinforcing—just doing it makes the dog feel better in some way, whether you are there to say "good boy!" or not. Some examples are eating garbage, pulling the stuffing out of your sofa, barking at passersby, or urinating on the floor.

Although you don't want to personally punish your dog, the occasional deterrent may be called for to help derail these kinds of self-rewarding misbehaviors. In these cases, mild forms of impersonal or remote punishment can be used as part of a correction. The goal isn't to make your dog feel bad or to "know he has done wrong," but to help redirect him to alternate behaviors that are more acceptable to you.

The Problems with Personal Punishment

- Personally punished dogs are not taught appropriate behaviors.
- Personally punished dogs only stop misbehaving when they are caught or interrupted, but they don't learn not to misbehave when they are alone.
- Personally punished dogs become shy, fearful, and distrusting.
- Personally punished dogs may become defensively aggressive.
- Personally punished dogs become suppressed and inhibited.
- Personally punished dogs become stressed, triggering stress-reducing behaviors that their owners interpret as acts of spite, triggering even more punishment.
- Personally punished dogs have stressed owners.
- Personally punished dogs may begin to repeat behaviors they have been taught will result in negative, but predictable, attention.
- Personally punished dogs are more likely to be given away than are positively trained dogs.

You do this by pairing a slightly startling, totally impersonal sound with an equally impersonal and *very mild* remote consequence. The impersonal sound might be a single shake of an empty plastic pop bottle with pennies in it, held out of your dog's sight. Or you could use a vocal expression such as "eh!" delivered with you looking *away* from your misbehaving dog.

Pair your chosen sound—the penny bottle or "eh!"—with either a slight tug on his collar or a sneaky spritz on the rump from a water bottle. Do this right *as* he touches something he should not; bad timing will confuse your dog and undermine your training success.

To keep things under your control and make sure you get the timing right, it's best to do this as a setup. "Accidentally" drop a shoe on the floor, and then help your dog learn some things are best avoided. As he sniffs the shoe say "eh!" without looking at him and give a *slight* tug against his collar. This sound will quickly become meaningful as a correction all by itself—sometimes after just one setup—making the tug correction obsolete. The tug lets your dog see that you were right; going for that shoe *was* a bad idea! Your wise dog will be more likely to heed your warning next time, and probably move closer to you where it's safe. Be a good friend and pick up the nasty shoe. He'll be relieved and you'll look heroic. Later, when he's home alone and encounters a stray shoe, he'll want to give it a wide berth.

Your negative marking sound will come in handy in the future, when your dog begins to venture down the wrong behavioral path. The goal is not to announce your disapproval or to threaten your dog. You are not telling him to stop or showing how *you* feel about his behavior. You are sounding a warning to a friend who's venturing off toward danger—"I wouldn't if I were you!" Suddenly, there is an abrupt, rather startling, noise! Now is the moment to redirect him and help him earn positive reinforcement. That interrupted behavior will become something he wants to avoid in the future, but he won't want to avoid you.

Practical Commands for Family Pets

Before you begin training your dog, let's look at some equipment you'll want to have on hand:

- **A buckle collar** is fine for most dogs. If your dog pulls *very* hard, try a head collar, a device similar to a horse halter that helps reduce pulling by turning the dog's head. *Do not* use a choke chain (sometimes called a training collar), because they cause physical harm even when used correctly.
- **Six-foot training leash and twenty-six–foot retractable leash.**
- **A few empty plastic soda bottles with about twenty pennies in each one.** This will be used to impersonally interrupt misbehaviors before redirecting dogs to more positive activities.
- **A favorite squeaky toy,** to motivate, attract attention, and reward your dog during training.

Lure your dog to take just a few steps with you on the leash by being inviting and enthusiastic. Make sure you reward him for his efforts.

Baby Steps

Allow your young pup to drag a short, lightweight leash attached to a buckle collar for a few *supervised* moments, several times each day. At first the leash may annoy him and he may jump around a bit trying to get away from it. Distract him with your squeaky toy or a bit of his kibble and he'll quickly get used to his new "tail."

Begin walking him on the leash by holding the end and following him. As he adapts, you can begin to assert gentle direct pressure to teach him to follow you. Don't jerk or yank, or he will become afraid to walk when the leash is on. If he becomes hesitant, squat down facing him and let him figure out that by moving toward you he is safe and secure. If he remains confused or frightened and doesn't come to you, go to him and help him understand that you provide safe harbor while he's on the leash. Then back away a few steps and try again to lure him to you. As he learns that you are the "home base," he'll want to follow when you walk a few steps, waiting for you to stop, squat down, and make him feel great.

So Attached to You!

The next step in training your dog—and this is a very important one—is to begin spending at least an hour or more each day with him on a four- to six-foot leash, held by or tethered to you. This training will increase his attachment to you—literally!—as you sit quietly or walk about, tending to your household business. When you are quiet, he'll learn it is time to settle; when you are active, he'll learn to move with you. Tethering also keeps him out of trouble when you are busy but still want his company. It is a great alternative to confining a dog, and can be used instead of crating any time you're home and need to slow him down a bit.

Rotating your dog from supervised freedom to tethered time to some quiet time in the crate or his gated area gives him a diverse and balanced day while he is learning. Two confined or tethered hours is the most you should require of your dog in one stretch, before changing to some supervised freedom, play, or a walk.

The dog in training may, at times, be stressed by all of the changes he is dealing with. Provide a stress outlet, such as a toy to chew on, when he is confined or tethered. He will settle into his quiet time more quickly and completely. Always be sure to provide several rounds of daily play and free time (in a fenced area or on your retractable leash) in addition to plenty of chewing materials.

Dog Talk

Dogs don't speak in words, but they do have a language—body language. They use postures, vocalizations, movements, facial gestures,

Tethering your dog is great way to keep him calm and under control, but still with you.

odors, and touch—usually with their mouths—to communicate what they are feeling and thinking.

We also "speak" using body language. We have quite an array of postures, movements, and facial gestures that accompany our touch and language as we attempt to communicate with our pets. And our dogs can quickly figure us out!

Alone, without associations, words are just noises. But, because we pair them with meaningful body language, our dogs make the connection. Dogs can really learn to understand much of what we *say*, if what we *do* at the same time is consistent.

The Positive Marker

Start your dog's education with one of the best tricks in dog training: Pair various positive reinforcers—food, a toy, touch—with a sound such as a click on a clicker (which you can get at the pet supply store) or a spoken word like "good!" or "yes!" This will enable you to later "mark" your dog's desirable behaviors.

It seems too easy: Just say "yes!" and give the dog his toy. (Or use whatever sound and reward you have chosen.) Later, when you make your marking sound right at the instant your dog does the right thing, he will know you are going to be giving him something good for that particular action. And he'll be eager to repeat the behavior to hear you mark it again!

Next, you must teach your dog to understand the meaning of cues you'll be using to ask him to perform specific behaviors. This is easy, too. Does he already do things you might like him to do on command? Of course! He lies down, he sits, he picks things up, he drops them again, he comes to you. All of the behaviors you'd like to control are already part of your dog's natural repertoire. The trick is getting him to offer those behaviors when you ask for them. And that means you have to teach him to associate a particular behavior on his part with a particular behavior on your part.

Sit Happens

Teach your dog an important new rule: From now on, he is only touched and petted when he is either sitting or lying down. You won't need to ask him to sit; in fact, you should not. Just keeping him tethered near you so there isn't much to do but stand, be ignored, or settle, and wait until sit happens.

He may pester you a bit, but be stoic and unresponsive. Starting now, when *you* are sitting down, a sitting dog is the only one you see and pay attention to. He will eventually sit, and as he does, attach the word "sit"—but don't be too excited or he'll jump right back up. Now mark with your positive sound that promises something good, then reward him with a slow, quiet, settling pet.

Training requires consistent reinforcement. Ask others to also wait until your dog is sitting and calm to touch him, and he will associate being petted with being relaxed. Be sure you train your dog to associate everyone's touch with quiet bonding.

Reinforcing "Sit" as a Command

Since your dog now understands one concept of working for a living—sit to earn petting—you can begin to shape and reinforce his desire to sit. Hold toys, treats, his bowl of food, and turn into a statue. But don't prompt him to sit! Instead, remain frozen and unavailable, looking somewhere out into space, over his head. He will put on a bit of a show, trying to get a response from you, and may offer various behaviors, but only one will push your button—sitting. Wait for him to offer the "right" behavior, and when he does, you unfreeze. Say "sit," then mark with an excited "good!" and give him the toy or treat with a release command—"OK!"

When you notice spontaneous sits occurring, be sure to take advantage of those free opportunities to make your command sequence meaningful and positive. Say "sit" as you observe sit happen—then mark with "good!" and praise, pet, or reward the dog. Soon, every time you look at your dog he'll be sitting and looking right back at you!

Now, after thirty days of purely positive practice, it's time to give him a test. When he is just walking around doing his own thing, suddenly ask him to sit. He'll probably do it right away. If he doesn't, do *not* repeat your command, or you'll just undermine its meaning ("sit" means sit *now;* the command is not "sit, sit, sit, sit"). Instead, get something he likes and let him know you have it. Wait for him to offer the sit—he will—then say "sit!" and complete your marking and rewarding sequence.

OK

"OK" will probably rate as one of your dog's favorite words. It's like the word "recess" to schoolchildren. It is the word used to release your dog from a command. You can introduce "OK" during your "sit" practice. When he gets up from a sit, say "OK" to tell him the sitting is finished. Soon that sound will mean "freedom."

Make it even more meaningful and positive. Whenever he spontaneously bounds away, say "OK!" Squeak a toy, and when he notices and shows interest, toss it for him.

Down

I've mentioned that you should only pet your dog when he is either sitting or lying down. Now, using the approach I've just introduced for "sit," teach your dog to lie down. You will be a statue, and hold something he would like to get but that you'll only release to a dog who is lying down. It helps to lower the desired item to the floor in front of him, still not speaking and not letting him have it until he offers you the new behavior you are seeking.

Lower your dog's reward to the floor to help him figure out what behavior will earn him his reward.

He may offer a sit and then wait expectantly, but you must make him keep searching for the new trick that triggers your generosity. Allow your dog to experiment and find the right answer, even if he has to search around for it first. When he lands on "down" and learns it is another behavior that works, he'll offer it more quickly the next time.

Don't say "down" until he lies down, to tightly associate your prompt with the correct behavior. To say "down, down, down" as he is sitting, looking at you, or pawing at the toy would make "down" mean those behaviors instead! Whichever behavior he offers, a training opportunity has been created. Once you've attached and shaped both sitting and lying down, you can ask for both behaviors with your verbal prompts, "sit" or "down." Be sure to only reinforce the "correct" reply!

Stay

"Stay" can easily be taught as an extension of what you've already been practicing. To teach "stay," you follow the entire sequence for reinforcing a "sit" or "down," except you wait a bit longer before you give the release word, "OK!" Wait a second or two longer during each practice before saying "OK!" and releasing your dog to the positive reinforcer (toy, treat, or one of life's other rewards).

You can step on the leash to help your dog understand the down-stay, but only do this when he is already lying down. You don't want to hurt him!

If he gets up before you've said "OK," you have two choices: pretend the release was your idea and quickly interject "OK!" as he breaks; or, if he is more experienced and practiced, mark the behavior with your correction sound—"eh!"— and then gently put him back on the spot, wait for him to lie down, and begin again. Be sure the next three practices are a success. Ask him to wait for just a second, and release him before he can be wrong. You need to keep your dog feeling like more of a success than a failure as you begin to test his training in increasingly more distracting and difficult situations.

As he gets the hang of it—he stays until you say "OK"— you can gradually push for longer times—up to a minute on a sit-stay, and up to three minutes on a down-stay. You can also gradually add distractions and work in new environments. To add a minor self-correction for the down-stay, stand on the dog's leash after he lies down, allowing about three inches of slack. If tries to get up before you've said "OK," he'll discover it doesn't work.

Do not step on the leash to make your dog lie down! This could badly hurt his neck, and will destroy his trust in you. Remember, we are teaching our dogs to make the best choices, not inflicting our answers upon them!

Come

Rather than thinking of "come" as an action—"come to me"—think of it as a place—"the dog is sitting in front of me, facing me." Since your dog by now really likes sitting to earn your touch and other positive reinforcement, he's likely to sometimes sit directly in front of you, facing you, all on his own. When this happens, give it a specific name: "come."

Now follow the rest of the training steps you have learned to make him like doing it and reinforce the behavior by practicing it any chance you get. Anything your dog wants and likes could be earned as a result of his first offering the sit-in-front known as "come."

You can help guide him into the right location. Use your hands as "landing gear" and pat the insides of your legs at his nose level. Do this while backing up a bit, to help him maneuver to the straight-in-front, facing-you position. Don't say the

Pat the insides of your legs to show your dog exactly where you like him to sit when you say "come."

word "come" while he's maneuvering, because he hasn't! You are trying to make "come" the end result, not the work in progress.

You can also help your dog by marking his movement in the right direction: Use your positive sound or word to promise he is getting warm. When he finally sits facing you, enthusiastically say "come," mark again with your positive word, and release him with an enthusiastic "OK!" Make it so worth his while, with lots of play and praise, that he can't wait for you to ask him to come again!

Building a Better Recall

Practice, practice, practice. Now, practice some more. Teach your dog that all good things in life hinge upon him first sitting in front of you in a behavior named "come." When you think he really has got it, test him by asking him to "come" as you gradually add distractions and change locations. Expect setbacks as you make these changes and practice accordingly. Lower your expectations and make his task easier so he is able to get it right. Use those distractions as rewards, when they are appropriate. For example, let him check out the interesting leaf that blew by as a reward for first coming to you and ignoring it.

Add distance and call your dog to come while he is on his retractable leash. If he refuses and sits looking at you blankly, *do not* jerk, tug, "pop," or reel him in. Do nothing! It is his move; wait to see what behavior he offers. He'll either begin to approach (mark the behavior with an excited "good!"), sit and do nothing (just keep waiting), or he'll try to move in some direction other than toward you. If he tries to leave, use your correction marker—"eh!"— and bring him to a stop by letting him walk to the end of the leash, *not* by jerking him. Now walk to him in a neutral manner, and don't jerk or show any disapproval. Gently bring him back to the spot where he was when you called him, then back away and face him, still waiting and not reissuing your command. Let him keep examining his options until he finds the one that works—yours!

If you have practiced everything I've suggested so far and given your dog a chance to really learn what "come" means, he is well aware of what you want and is quite intelligently weighing all his options. The only way he'll know your way is the one that works is to be allowed to examine his other choices and discover that they *don't* work.

Sooner or later every dog tests his training. Don't be offended or angry when your dog tests you. No matter how positive you've made it, he won't always want to do everything you ask, every time. When he explores the "what happens if I don't" scenario, your training is being strengthened. He will discover through his own process of trial and error that the best—and only—way out of a command he really doesn't feel compelled to obey is to obey it.

Let's Go

Many pet owners wonder if they can retain control while walking their dogs and still allow at least some running in front, sniffing, and playing. You might worry that allowing your dog occasional freedom could result in him expecting it all the time, leading to a testy, leash-straining walk. It's possible for both parties on the leash to have an enjoyable experience by implementing and reinforcing well-thought-out training techniques.

Begin by making word associations you'll use on your walks. Give the dog some slack on the leash, and as he starts to walk away from you say "OK" and begin to follow him.

Give your dog slack on his leash as you walk and let him make the decision to walk with you.

Do not let him drag you; set the pace even when he is being given a turn at being the leader. Whenever he starts to pull, just come to a standstill and refuse to move (or refuse to allow him to continue forward) until there is slack in the leash. Do this correction without saying anything at all. When he isn't pulling, you may decide to just stand still and let him sniff about within the range the slack leash allows, or you may even mosey along following him. After a few minutes of "recess," it is time to work. Say something like "that's it" or "time's up," close the distance between you and your dog, and touch him.

Next say "let's go" (or whatever command you want to use to mean "follow me as we walk"). Turn and walk off, and, if he follows, mark his behavior with "good!" Then stop,

When your dog catches up with you, make sure you let him know what a great dog he is!

Intersperse periods of attentive walking, where your dog is on a shorter leash, with periods on a slack leash, where he is allowed to look and sniff around.

squat down, and let him catch you. Make him glad he did! Start again, and do a few transitions as he gets the hang of your follow-the-leader game, speeding up, slowing down, and trying to make it fun. When you stop, he gets to catch up and receive some deserved positive reinforcement. Don't forget that's the reason he is following you, so be sure to make it worth his while!

Require him to remain attentive to you. Do not allow sniffing, playing, eliminating, or pulling during your time as leader on a walk. If he seems to get distracted—which, by the way, is the main reason dogs walk poorly with their people—change direction or pace without saying a word. Just help him realize "oops, I lost track of my human." Do not jerk his neck and say "heel"—this will make the word "heel" mean pain in the neck and will not encourage him to cooperate with you. Don't repeat "let's go," either. He needs to figure out that it is his job to keep track of and follow you if he wants to earn the positive benefits you provide.

The best reward you can give a dog for performing an attentive, controlled walk is a few minutes of walking without all of the controls. Of course, he must remain on a leash even during the "recess" parts of the walk, but allowing him to discriminate between attentive following—"let's go"—and having a few moments of relaxation—"OK"—will increase his willingness to work.

Training for Attention

Your dog pretty much has a one-track mind. Once he is focused on something, everything else is excluded. This can be great, for instance, when he's focusing on you! But it can also be dangerous if, for example, his attention is riveted on the bunny he is chasing and he does not hear you call—that is, not unless he has been trained to pay attention when you say his name.

When you say your dog's name, you'll want him to make eye contact with you. Begin teaching this by making yourself so intriguing that he can't help but look.

When you call your dog's name, you will again be seeking a specific response—eye contact. The best way to teach this is to trigger his alerting response by making a noise with your mouth, such as whistling or a kissing sound, and then immediately doing something he'll find very intriguing.

You can play a treasure hunt game to help teach him to regard his name as a request for attention. As a bonus, you can reinforce the rest of his new vocabulary at the same time.

Treasure Hunt

Make a kissing sound, then jump up and find a dog toy or dramatically raid the fridge and rather noisily eat a piece of cheese. After doing this twice, make a kissing sound and then look at your dog.

Of course he is looking at you! He is waiting to see if that sound—the kissing sound—means you're going to go hunting again. After all, you're so good at it! Because he is looking, say his name, mark with "good," then go hunting and find his toy. Release it to him with an "OK." At any point if he follows you, attach your "let's go!" command; if he leaves you, give permission with "OK."

Using this approach, he cannot be wrong—any behavior your dog offers can be named. You can add things like "take it" when he picks up a toy, and "thank you" when he happens to drop one. Many opportunities to make your new vocabulary meaningful and positive can be found within this simple training game.

Problems to watch out for when teaching the treasure hunt:

- You really do not want your dog to come to you when you call his name (later, when you try to engage his attention to ask him to stay, he'll already be on his way toward you). You just want him to look at you.
- Saying "watch me, watch me" doesn't teach your dog to *offer* his attention. It just makes you a background noise.
- Don't lure your dog's attention with the reward. Get his attention and then reward him for looking. Try holding a toy in one hand with your arm stretched out to your side. Wait until he looks at you rather than the toy. Now say his name then mark with "good!" and release the toy. As he goes for it, say "OK."

To get your dog's attention, try holding his toy with your arm out to your side. Wait until he looks at you, then mark the moment and give him the toy.

Teaching Cooperation

Never punish your dog for failing to obey you or try to punish him into compliance. Bribing, repeating yourself, and doing a behavior for him all avoid the real issue of dog training—his will. He must be helped to be willing, not made to achieve tasks. Good dog training helps your dog want to obey. He learns that he can gain what he values most through cooperation and compliance, and can't gain those things any other way.

Your dog is learning to *earn,* rather than expect, the good things in life. And you've become much more important to him than you were before. Because you are allowing him to experiment and learn, he doesn't have to be forced, manipulated, or bribed. When he wants something, he can gain it by cooperating with you. One of those "somethings"—and a great reward you shouldn't underestimate—is your positive attention, paid to him with love and sincere approval!

Chapter 10

Housetraining Your Bichon Frise

Excerpted from Housetraining: An Owner's Guide to a Happy Healthy Pet, *1st Edition, by September Morn*

By the time puppies are about 3 weeks old, they start to follow their mother around. When they are a few steps away from their clean sleeping area, the mama dog stops. The pups try to nurse but mom won't allow it. The pups mill around in frustration, then nature calls and they all urinate and defecate here, away from their bed. The mother dog returns to the nest, with her brood waddling behind her. Their first housetraining lesson has been a success.

The next one to housetrain puppies should be their breeder. The breeder watches as the puppies eliminate, then deftly removes the soiled papers and replaces them with clean papers before the pups can traipse back through their messes. He has wisely arranged the puppies' space so their bed, food, and drinking water are as far away from the elimination area as possible. This way, when the pups follow their mama, they will move away from their sleeping and eating area before eliminating. This habit will help the pups be easily housetrained.

Your Housetraining Shopping List

While your puppy's mother and breeder are getting her started on good housetraining habits, you'll need to do some shopping. If you have all the essentials in place before your dog arrives, it will be easier to help her learn the rules from day one.

Newspaper: The younger your puppy and larger her breed, the more newspapers you'll need. Newspaper is absorbent, abundant, cheap, and convenient.

Puddle Pads: If you prefer not to stockpile newspaper, a commercial alternative is puddle pads. These thick paper pads can be purchased under several trade names at pet supply stores. The pads have waterproof backing, so puppy urine doesn't seep through onto the floor. Their disadvantages are that they will cost you more than newspapers and that they contain plastics that are not biodegradable.

Poop Removal Tool: There are several types of poop removal tools available. Some are designed with a separate pan and rake, and others have the handles hinged like scissors. Some scoops need two hands for operation, while others are designed for one-handed use. Try out the different brands at your pet supply store. Put a handful of pebbles or dog kibble on the floor and then pick them up with each type of scoop to determine which works best for you.

Plastic Bags: When you take your dog outside your yard, you *must* pick up after her. Dog waste is unsightly, smelly, and can harbor disease. In many cities and towns, the law mandates dog owners clean up pet waste deposited on public ground. Picking up after your dog using a plastic bag scoop is simple. Just put your hand inside the bag, like a mitten, and then grab the droppings. Turn the bag inside out, tie the top, and that's that.

Crate: To housetrain a puppy, you will need some way to confine her when you're unable to supervise. A dog crate is a secure way to confine your dog for short periods during the day and to use as a comfortable bed at night. Crates come in wire mesh and in plastic. The wire ones are foldable to store flat in a smaller space. The plastic ones are more cozy, draft-free, and quiet, and are approved for airline travel.

Baby Gates: Since you shouldn't crate a dog for more than an hour or two at a time during the day, baby gates are a good way to limit your dog's freedom in the house. Be sure the baby gates you use are safe. The old-fashioned wooden, expanding lattice type has seriously injured a number of children by collapsing and trapping a leg, arm, or neck. That type of gate can hurt a puppy, too, so use the modern grid type gates instead. You'll need more than one baby gate if you have several doorways to close off.

Exercise Pen: Portable exercise pens are great when you have a young pup or a small dog. These metal or plastic pens are made of rectangular panels that are hinged together. The pens are freestanding, sturdy, foldable, and can be carried like a suitcase. You could set one up in your kitchen as the pup's daytime corral, and then take it outdoors to contain your pup while you garden or just sit and enjoy the day.

Enzymatic Cleaner: All dogs make housetraining mistakes. Accept this and be ready for it by buying an enzymatic cleaner made especially for pet accidents. Dogs like to eliminate where they have done it before, and lingering smells lead them to those spots. Ordinary household cleaners may remove all the odors you can smell, but only an enzymatic cleaner will remove everything your dog can smell.

A portable exercise pen like this one is a great choice for an indoor corral.

> ## Don't Overuse the Crate
>
> A crate serves well as a dog's overnight bed, but you should not leave the dog in her crate for more than an hour or two during the day. Throughout the day, she needs to play and exercise. She is likely to want to drink some water and will undoubtedly eliminate. Confining your dog all day will give her no option but to soil her crate. This is not just unpleasant for you and the dog, but it reinforces bad cleanliness habits. And crating a pup for the whole day is abusive. Don't do it.

The First Day

Housetraining is a matter of establishing good habits in your dog. That means you never want her to learn anything she will eventually have to unlearn. Start off housetraining on the right foot by teaching your dog that you prefer her to eliminate outside. Designate a potty area in your backyard (if you have one) or in the street in front of your home and take your dog to it as soon as you arrive home. Let her sniff a bit and, when she squats to go, give the action a name: "potty" or "do it" or anything else you won't be embarrassed to say in public. Eventually your dog will associate that word with the act and will eliminate on command. When she's finished, praise her with "good potty!"

That first day, take your puppy out to the potty area frequently. Although she may not eliminate every time, you are establishing a routine: You take her to her spot, ask her to eliminate, and praise her when she does.

Just before bedtime, take your dog to her potty area once more. Stand by and wait until she produces. Do not put your dog to bed for the night until she has eliminated. Be patient and calm. This is not the time to play with or excite your dog. If she's too excited, a pup not only won't eliminate, she probably won't want to sleep either.

Most dogs, even young ones, will not soil their beds if they can avoid it. For this reason, a sleeping crate can be a tremendous help during housetraining. Being crated at night can help a dog develop the muscles that control elimination. So after your dog has emptied out, put her to bed in her crate.

A good place to put your dog's sleeping crate is near your own bed. Dogs are pack animals, so they feel safer sleeping with others in a common area. In your

Housetraining is a matter of establishing good habits right from the start. The very first day, take your puppy to her elimination spot and praise her when she goes.

bedroom, the pup will be near you and you'll be close enough to hear when she wakes during the night and needs to eliminate.

Pups under 4 months old often are not able to hold their urine all night. If your puppy has settled down to sleep but awakens and fusses a few hours later, she probably needs to go out. For the best housetraining progress, take your pup to her elimination area whenever she needs to go, even in the wee hours of the morning.

Your pup may soil in her crate if you ignore her late night urgency. It's unfair to let this happen, and it sends the wrong message about your expectations for cleanliness. Resign yourself to this midnight outing and just get up and take the pup out. Your pup will outgrow this need soon and will learn in the process that she can count on you, and you'll wake happily each morning to a clean dog.

The next morning, the very first order of business is to take your pup out to eliminate. Don't forget to take her to her special potty spot, ask her to eliminate, and then praise her when she does. After your pup empties out in the morning, give her breakfast, and then take her to her potty area again. After that, she shouldn't need to eliminate again right away, so you can allow her some free playtime. Keep an eye on the pup though, because when she pauses in play she may need to go potty. Take her to the right spot, give the command, and praise if she produces.

Confine Your Pup

A pup or dog who has not finished housetraining should *never* be allowed the run of the house unattended. A new dog (especially a puppy) with unlimited access to your house will make her own choices about where to eliminate. Vigilance during your new dog's first few weeks in your home will pay big dividends. Every potty mistake delays housetraining progress; every success speeds it along.

Prevent problems by setting up a controlled environment for your new pet. A good place for a puppy corral is often the kitchen. Kitchens almost always have waterproof or easily cleaned floors, which is a distinct asset with leaky pups. A bathroom, laundry room, or enclosed porch could be used for a puppy corral, but the kitchen is generally the best location. Kitchens are a meeting place and a hub of activity for many families, and a puppy will learn better manners when she is socialized thoroughly with family, friends, and nice strangers.

The way you structure your pup's corral area is very important. Her bed, food, and water should be at the opposite end of the corral from the potty area. When you first get your pup, spread newspaper over the rest of the floor of her playpen corral. Lay the papers at least four pages thick and be sure to overlap the edges. As you note the pup's progress, you can remove the papers nearest the sleeping and eating corner. Gradually decrease the size of the papered area until only the end where you want the pup to eliminate is covered. If you will be training your dog to eliminate outside, place newspaper at the end of the corral that is closest to the door that leads outdoors. That way as she moves away from the clean area to the papered area, the pup will also form the habit of heading toward the door to go out.

Maintain a scent marker for the pup's potty area by reserving a small soiled piece of paper when you clean up. Place this piece, with her scent of urine, under the top sheet of the clean papers you spread. This will cue your pup where to eliminate.

Most dog owners use a combination of indoor papers and outdoor

> ### T I P
>
> **Water**
>
> Make sure your dog has access to clean water at all times. Limiting the amount of water a dog drinks is not necessary for housetraining success and can be very dangerous. A dog needs water to digest food, to maintain a proper body temperature and proper blood volume, and to clean her system of toxins and wastes. A healthy dog will automatically drink the right amount. Do not restrict water intake. Controlling your dog's access to water is not the key to housetraining her; controlling her access to everything else in your home is.

Take your pup to her outdoor potty place frequently throughout the day. Keep her leashed so she won't just wander around.

elimination areas. When the pup is left by herself in the corral, she can potty on the ever-present newspaper. When you are available to take the pup outside, she can do her business in the outdoor spot. It is not difficult to switch a pup from indoor paper training to outdoor elimination. Owners of large pups often switch early, but potty papers are still useful if the pup spends time in her indoor corral while you're away. Use the papers as long as your pup needs them. If you come home and they haven't been soiled, you are ahead.

When setting up your pup's outdoor yard, put the lounging area as far away as possible from the potty area, just as with the indoor corral setup. People with large yards, for example, might leave a patch unmowed at the edge of the lawn to serve as the dog's elimination area. Other dog owners teach the dog to relieve herself in a designated corner of a deck or patio. For an apartment-dwelling city dog, the outdoor potty area might be a tiny balcony or the curb. Each dog owner has somewhat different expectations for their dog. Teach your dog to eliminate in a spot that suits your environment and lifestyle.

Be sure to pick up droppings in your yard at least once a day. Dogs have a natural desire to stay far away from their own excrement, and if too many piles litter the ground, your dog won't want to walk through it and will start eliminating elsewhere. Leave just one small piece of feces in the potty area to remind your dog where the right spot is located.

To help a pup adapt to the change from indoors to outdoors, take one of her potty papers outside to the new elimination area. Let the pup stand on the paper when she goes potty outdoors. Each day for four days, reduce the size of the paper by half. By the fifth day, the pup, having used a smaller and smaller piece of paper to stand on, will probably just go to that spot and eliminate.

Take your pup to her outdoor potty place frequently throughout the day. A puppy can hold her urine for only about as many hours as her age in months, and will move her bowels as many times a day as she eats. So a 2-month-old pup will urinate about every two hours, while at 4 months she can manage about four hours between piddles. Pups vary somewhat in their rate of development, so this is not a hard and fast rule. It does, however, present a realistic idea of how long a pup can be left without access to a potty place. Past 4 months, her potty trips will be less frequent.

When you take the dog outdoors to her spot, keep her leashed so that she won't wander away. Stand quietly and let her sniff around in the designated area. If your pup starts to leave before she has eliminated, gently lead her back and remind her to go. If your pup sniffs at the spot, praise her calmly, say the command word, and just wait. If she produces, praise serenely, then give her time to sniff around a little more. She may not be finished, so give her time to go again before allowing her to play and explore her new home.

If you find yourself waiting more than five minutes for your dog to potty, take her back inside. Watch your pup carefully for twenty minutes, not giving her any opportunity to slip away to eliminate unnoticed. If you are too busy to watch the pup, put her in her crate. After twenty minutes, take her to the outdoor potty spot again and tell her what to do. If you're unsuccessful after five minutes, crate the dog again. Give her another chance to eliminate in fifteen or twenty minutes. Eventually, she will have to go.

Watch Your Pup

Be vigilant and don't let the pup make a mistake in the house. Each time you successfully anticipate elimination and take your pup to the potty spot, you'll move a step closer to your goal. Stay aware of your puppy's needs. If you ignore the pup, she will make mistakes and you'll be cleaning up more messes.

Keep a chart of your new dog's elimination behavior for the first three or four days. Jot down what times she eats, sleeps, and eliminates. After several days a pattern will emerge that can help you determine your pup's body rhythms. Most dogs tend to eliminate at fairly regular intervals. Once you know your new dog's natural rhythms, you'll be able to anticipate her needs and schedule appropriate potty outings.

Understanding the meanings of your dog's postures can also help you win the battle of the puddle. When your dog is getting ready to eliminate, she will display a specific set of postures. The sooner you can learn to read these signals, the cleaner your floor will stay.

A young puppy who feels the urge to eliminate may start to sniff the ground and walk in a circle. If the pup is very young, she may simply squat and go. All young puppies, male or female, squat to urinate. If you are housetraining a pup under 4 months of age, regardless of sex, watch for the beginnings of a squat as the signal to rush the pup to the potty area.

Try not to let your pup make a mistake in the house. Be alert to her signals that she needs to go out.

When a puppy is getting ready to defecate, she may run urgently back and forth or turn in a circle while sniffing or starting to squat. If defecation is imminent, the pup's anus may protrude or open slightly. When she starts to go, the pup will squat and hunch her back, her tail sticking straight out behind. There is no mistaking this posture; nothing else looks like this. If your pup takes this position, take her to her potty area. Hurry! You may have to carry her to get there in time.

A young puppy won't have much time between feeling the urge and actually eliminating, so you'll have to be quick to note her postural clues and intercept your pup in time. Pups from 3 to 6 months have a few seconds more between the urge and the act than younger ones do. The older your pup, the more time you'll have to get her to the potty area after she begins the posture signals that alert you to her need.

Accidents Happen

If you see your pup about to eliminate somewhere other than the designated area, interrupt her immediately. Say "wait, wait, wait!" or clap your hands loudly to startle her into stopping. Carry the pup, if she's still small enough, or take her collar and lead her to the correct area. Once your dog is in the potty area, give her the command to eliminate. Use a friendly voice for the command, then wait patiently for her to produce. The pup may be tense because you've just startled her and may have to relax a bit before she's able to eliminate. When she does her job, include the command word in the praise you give ("good potty").

The old-fashioned way of housetraining involved punishing a dog's mistakes even before she knew what she was supposed to do. Puppies were punished for breaking rules they didn't understand about functions they couldn't control. This was not fair. While your dog is new to housetraining, there is no need or excuse for punishing her mistakes. Your job is to take the dog to the potty area just before she needs to go, especially with pups under 3 months old. If you aren't watching your pup closely enough and she has an accident, don't punish the puppy for your failure to anticipate her needs. It's not the pup's fault; it's yours.

In any case, punishment is not an effective tool for housetraining most dogs. Many will react to punishment by hiding puddles and feces where you won't find them right away (like behind the couch or under the desk). This eventually may lead to punishment after the fact, which leads to more hiding, and so on.

Instead of punishing for mistakes, stay a step ahead of potty accidents by learning to anticipate your pup's needs. Accompany your dog to the designated

A baby puppy does not have the physical ability to control her bladder and bowels for very long. Please don't expect more from your dog than she can do.

potty area when she needs to go. Tell her what you want her to do and praise her when she goes. This will work wonders. Punishment won't be necessary if you are a good teacher.

What happens if you come upon a mess after the fact? Some trainers say a dog can't remember having eliminated, even a few moments after she has done so. This is not true. The fact is that urine and feces carry a dog's unique scent, which she (and every other dog) can instantly recognize. So, if you happen upon a potty mistake after the fact you can still use it to teach your dog.

But remember, no punishment! Spanking, hitting, shaking, or scaring a puppy for having a housetraining accident is confusing and counterproductive. Spend your energy instead on positive forms of teaching.

Take your pup and a paper towel to the mess. Point to the urine or feces and calmly tell your puppy, "no potty here." Then scoop or sop up the accident with the paper towel. Take the evidence and the pup to the approved potty area. Drop the mess on the ground and tell the dog, "good potty here," as if she had done the deed in the right place. If your pup sniffs at the evidence, praise her calmly. If the accident happened very recently your dog may not have to go yet, but wait with her a few minutes anyway. If she eliminates, praise her. Afterwards, go finish cleaning up the mess.

Soon the puppy will understand that there is a place where you are pleased about elimination and other places where you are not. Praising for elimination in the approved place will help your pup remember the rules.

Scheduling Basics

With a new puppy in the home, don't be surprised if your rising time is suddenly a little earlier than you've been accustomed to. Puppies have earned a reputation as very early risers. When your pup wakes you at the crack of dawn, you will have to get up and take her to her elimination spot. Be patient. When your dog is an adult, she may enjoy sleeping in as much as you do.

At the end of the chapter, you'll find a typical housetraining schedule for puppies aged 10 weeks to 6 months. (To find schedules for younger and older pups, and for adult dogs, visit this book's companion web site.) It's fine to adjust the rising times when using this schedule, but you should not adjust the intervals between feedings and potty outings unless your pup's behavior justifies a change. Your puppy can only meet your expectations in housetraining if you help her learn the rules.

Housetraining may seem like it takes up all your time at first. But as your dog gets older, she will learn to control herself.

The schedule for puppies is devised with the assumption that someone will be home most of the time with the pup. That would be the best scenario, of course, but is not always possible. You may be able to ease the problems of a latchkey pup by having a neighbor or friend look in on the pup at noon and take her to eliminate. A better solution might be hiring a pet sitter to drop by midday. A professional pet sitter will be knowledgeable about companion animals and can give your pup high-quality care and socialization. Some can even help train your pup in both potty manners and basic obedience. Ask your veterinarian and your dog-owning friends to recommend a good pet sitter.

If you must leave your pup alone during her early housetraining period, be sure to cover the entire floor of her corral with thick layers of overlapping newspaper. If you come home to messes in the puppy corral, just clean them up. Be patient—she's still a baby.

Use this schedule (and the ones on the companion web site) as a basic plan to help prevent housetraining accidents. Meanwhile, use your own powers of observation to discover how to best modify the basic schedule to fit your dog's unique needs. Each dog is an individual and will have her own rhythms, and each dog is reliable at a different age.

Schedule for Pups 10 Weeks to 6 Months

7:00 a.m.	Get up and take the puppy from her sleeping crate to her potty spot.
7:15	Clean up last night's messes, if any.
7:30	Food and fresh water.
7:45	Pick up the food bowl. Take the pup to her potty spot; wait and praise.
8:00	The pup plays around your feet while you have your breakfast.
9:00	Potty break (younger pups may not be able to wait this long).
9:15	Play and obedience practice.
10:00	Potty break.
10:15	The puppy is in her corral with safe toys to chew and play with.
11:30	Potty break (younger pups may not be able to wait this long).
11:45	Food and fresh water.
12:00 p.m.	Pick up the food bowl and take the pup to her potty spot.
12:15	The puppy is in her corral with safe toys to chew and play with.
1:00	Potty break (younger pups may not be able to wait this long).
1:15	Put the pup on a leash and take her around the house with you.
3:30	Potty break (younger pups may not be able to wait this long).
3:45	Put the pup in her corral with safe toys and chews for solitary play and/or a nap.
4:45	Potty break.
5:00	Food and fresh water.
5:15	Potty break.
5:30	The pup may play nearby (either leashed or in her corral) while you prepare your evening meal.

7:00	Potty break.
7:15	Leashed or closely watched, the pup may play and socialize with family and visitors.
9:15	Potty break (younger pups may not be able to wait this long).
10:45	Last chance to potty.
11:00	Put the pup to bed in her crate for the night.

Chapter 11

Your Bichon Frise and Your Family

A dding a dog automatically increases your family by one, no matter whether you live alone in an apartment or are part of a mother, father, and six kids household. The single-person family is fair game for numerous and varied canine misconceptions as to who is dog and who pays the bills, whereas a dog in a houseful of children will consider himself to be just one of the gang, littermates all. One dog and one child may give a dog reason to believe they are both kids or both dogs. Either interpretation requires parental supervision and sometimes speedy intervention.

As soon as one paw goes through the door into your home, your Bichon has to make many adjustments to become a part of your family. Your job is to make him fit in as painlessly as possible. An older dog may have some frame of reference from past experience, but to a 10-week-old puppy, everything is brand new: people, furniture, stairs, when and where people eat, sleep or watch TV, his own place and everyone else's space, smells, sounds, outdoors—everything!

Puppies, and newly acquired dogs of any age, do not need what we think of as "freedom." If you leave a new dog or puppy loose in the house, you will almost certainly return to find chaotic destruction and the dog will forever after equate your homecoming with a time of punishment to be dreaded. It is unfair to give your dog what amounts to "freedom to get into trouble." Instead, confine him to a crate for brief periods of your absence (up to three or four hours) and, for the long haul (a workday, for example), confine him to one untrashable area with his own toys, a bowl of water, and a radio left on (low) in another room.

The All-Adult Family

Most dogs in an adults-only household today are likely to be latchkey pets, with no one home all day but the dog. When you return after a tough day on the job, the dog can and should be your relaxation therapy. But going home can, instead, be a daily frustration.

Separation anxiety is a very common problem for a dog in a working household. It may begin with whines and barks of loneliness, but it will soon escalate into a frenzied destruction derby. That is why it is so important to set aside the time to teach a dog to relax when left alone in his confined area and to understand that he can trust you to return.

Let the dog get used to your work schedule in easy stages. Confine him to one room and go in and out of that room over and over again. Be casual about it. No physical, voice, or eye contact. When the pup no longer even notices your comings and goings, leave the house for varying lengths of time, returning to stay home for a few minutes and gradually increasing the time away. This training can take days, but the dog is learning that you haven't left him forever and that he can trust you.

Any time you leave the dog, but especially during this training period, be casual about your departure. No anxiety-building fond farewells. Just "bye" and go! Remember the "good dog" when you return to find everything more or less as you left it.

If things are a mess (or even a disaster) when you return, greet the dog, take him outside to eliminate, and then put him in his crate while you clean up. Rant and rave in the shower! *Do not* punish the dog. You were not there when it happened and the rule is: Only punish as you catch the dog in the act of wrongdoing. Obviously, it makes sense to get your latchkey puppy when you'll have a week or two to spend on these training essentials.

Family weekend activities should include your Bichon whenever possible. Depending on the pup's age, now is the time for a long walk in the park, playtime in the backyard, a hike in the woods. Socializing is as important as health care, good food, and physical exercise, so visiting Aunt Emma and Uncle Harry or the next-door neighbor's dog or cat is essential to developing an outgoing, friendly temperament in your pet.

If you are a single adult, socializing your dog at home and away will prevent him from becoming overly protective of you (or just overly attached), and will also prevent such behavioral problems as dominance and fear of strangers.

Babies

Whether already here or on the way, babies figure larger than life in the eyes of a dog. If the dog is there first, let him in on all your baby preparations in the house. When baby arrives, let your Bichon sniff any item of clothing that has been on the baby before Junior comes home. Then let Mom greet the dog first before introducing the new family member. Hold the baby down for the dog to see and sniff, but make sure someone's holding the dog on a leash in case of any sudden moves. Don't play keep-away or tease the dog with the baby, which only invites undesirable jumping up.

The dog and the baby are "family," and for starters can be treated almost as equals. Things rapidly change, however, especially when baby takes to creeping around on all fours on the dog's turf or, better yet, has yummy pudding all over her face and hands! That's when a lot of things in the dog's and baby's lives become more separate than equal.

Toddlers make terrible dog owners, but if you can't avoid the combination, use patient discipline (that is, positive teaching rather than punishment), and use time-outs before you run out of patience.

A dog and a baby (or a toddler, or an assertive young child) should never be left alone together. Take the dog with you or confine him. With a baby or youngster in the house, you'll have plenty of use for that wonderful canine safety device called a crate!

Young Children

Any dog in a house with kids will behave pretty much as the kids do, good or bad. But even good dogs and good children can get into trouble when play becomes rowdy and active.

Legs bobbing up and down, shrill voices screeching, a ball hurtling overhead, all add up to exuberant frustration for a dog who's just trying to be part of the gang. In a pack of puppies, any legs or toys being chased would be caught by a set of teeth, and all the pups involved would understand that is how the game is played. Kids do not understand this, nor do parents tolerate it. Bring the dog indoors before you have reason to regret it. This is time-out, not a punishment.

You can explain the situation to the children and tell them they must play quieter games until the puppy learns not to grab them with his mouth. Unfortunately, you can't explain it that easily to the dog. With adult supervision, they will learn how to play together.

Young children love to tease. Sticking their faces or wiggling their hands or fingers in the dog's face is teasing. To another person it might be just annoying, but it is threatening to a dog. There's another difference: We can make the child stop teasing with an explanation, but the only way a dog can stop it is with a warning growl and then with teeth. Teasing is the major cause of children being bitten by their pets. Treat it seriously.

Older Children

The best age for a child to get a first dog is between 8 and 12. That's when kids are able to accept some real responsibility for their pet. Even so, take the child's vow of "I will never ever forget to feed (brush, walk, and so on) the dog" for what it's worth: a child's good intention at that moment. Most kids today have extra lessons, soccer practice, Little League, ballet, and so forth piled on top of school schedules. There will be many times when Mom will have to come to the dog's rescue. "I walked the dog for you so you can set the table for me" is one way to get around a missed responsibility without laying on blame or guilt.

Kids in this age group make excellent obedience trainers because they are into the teaching/learning process themselves and they lack the self-consciousness of adults. Attending a dog show is something the whole family can enjoy, and watching Junior Showmanship may catch the eye of the kids. Older children can begin to get involved in many of the recreational activities that were reviewed in bonus chapter 1. Some of the agility obstacles, for example, can be set up in the backyard as a family project (with an adult making sure all the equipment is safe and secure for the dog).

Older kids are also beginning to look to the future and may envision themselves as veterinarians, trainers, show dog handlers, or writers of the next Lassie bestseller. Dogs are perfect confidants for these dreams. They won't tell a soul.

Other Pets

Introduce all pets tactfully. In a dog/cat situation, hold the dog, not the cat. Let two dogs meet on neutral turf—a stroll in the park or a walk down the street—with both on loose leashes to permit all the normal canine ways of saying hello, including routine sniffing, circling, more sniffing, and so on. Small creatures such as hamsters, chinchillas, or mice must be kept safe from their natural predators (dogs and cats).

Festive Family Occasions

Parties are great for people, but not necessarily for puppies. Until all the guests have arrived, put the dog in his crate or in a room where he won't be disturbed. A socialized dog can join the fun later, as long as he's not underfoot, annoying guests, or digging into the hors d'oeuvres.

There are a few dangers to consider, too. Doors opening and closing can allow a puppy to slip out unnoticed in the confusion, and you'll be organizing a search party instead of playing host or hostess. Party food and buffet service are not for dogs. Let your Bichon party in his crate with a nice big dog biscuit.

At Christmastime, not only are tree decorations dangerous and breakable (and perhaps family heirlooms), but extreme caution should be taken with the lights, cords, and outlets for the tree lights and any other festive lighting. Occasionally a dog lifts a leg, ignoring the fact that the tree is indoors. To avoid this, use a canine repellent, made for gardens, on the tree. Or keep him out of the tree room unless supervised. Whatever you do, *don't* invite trouble by hanging his toys (even new ones from Santa) on the tree!

Car Travel

Before you plan a vacation by car with your Bichon, be sure he enjoys car travel. Nothing spoils a holiday quicker than a carsick dog! Work within the dog's comfort level. Get in the car with the dog in his crate or attached to a canine car safety belt and just sit there until he relaxes. That's all. Next time, get in the car, turn on the engine, and go nowhere. Just sit. When that is okay, turn on the engine and go around the block. Now you can go for a ride and include a stop where you get out, leaving the dog for a minute or two.

On a cool or balmy day, always park in the shade and leave windows open several inches. And return quickly. On hot days, never leave your dog alone in the car; it only takes ten minutes for a car to become an overheated steel death trap.

Staying in Your RV

Walk through any RV campground and you'll see many fluffy white faces peering through RV windows. The Bichon seems made for RVing. Traveling via RV is great fun and easy for a Bichon; this breed is certainly the right size, doesn't take up much room, and doesn't shed. Barking is discouraged in most RV parks, though, so make sure you have kept up with your Bichon's training.

Motel or Pet Motel?

Not all motels or hotels accept pets, but you have a much better choice today than even a few years ago. To find a dog-friendly lodging, look at *On the Road Again with Man's Best Friend*, a series of directories that detail bed and breakfasts, inns, family resorts, and other hotels/motels. Some places require a refundable deposit to cover any damage incurred by the dog. More B&Bs accept pets now, but some restrict the size. That's another advantage of having a Bichon!

If taking your dog with you is not feasible, check out boarding kennels in your area. Your veterinarian may offer this service, or recommend a kennel or two they are familiar with. Go see the facilities for yourself, ask about exercise, diet, housing, and so on. Or, if you'd rather have your dog stay home, look into bonded pet sitters, many of whom will also bring in the mail and water your plants.

Find a Pet Sitter

To find an experienced, professional pet sitter in your area, check out the web sites of Pet Sitters International (www.petsit.com) and the National Association of Professional Pet Sitters (www.petsitters.org).

Appendix

Learning More About Your Bichon Frise

Some Good Books

Beauchamp. Richard G., *The Truth About Bichons*, American Cocker Magazine, 1998.
Heam, Ann, *The Proper Care of Bichon Frises*, TFH Publications, 2000.
Ransom, Jackie, *The Bichon Frise Today*, Howell Book House, 1999.
Stubbs, Barbara, *The Complete Bichon Frise*, Howell Book House, 1990.

About Health Care

Arden, Darlene, *The Angell Memorial Animal Hospital Book of Wellness and Preventive Care for Dogs*, Contemporary Books, 2003.
Bamberger, Michelle, DVM, *Help! The Quick Guide to First Aid for Your Dog*, Howell Book House, 1995.
Shojai, Amy, *Complete Care for Your Aging Dog*, New American Library, 2003.
Volhard, Wendy, and Kerry Brown, DVM, *Holistic Guide for a Healthy Dog*, Howell Book House, 2000.

About Training

McCullough, Susan, *Housetraining for Dummies*, Wiley Publishing, 2002.

Palika, Liz, *All Dogs Need Some Training*, Howell Book House, 1998.

Palika, Liz, *The KISS Guide to Raising a Puppy*, Dorling Kindersley, 2002.

Smith, Cheryl S., *The Rosetta Bone—the Key to Communication Between Humans and Canines*, Howell Book House, 2004.

Canine Activities

Burch, Mary, *Wanted: Animal Volunteers*, Howell Book House, 2002.

Hall, Lynn, *Dog Showing for Beginners*, Howell Book House, 1994.

O'Neil, Jacqueline F., *All About Agility*, Howell Book House, 1999.

Volhard, Jack and Wendy, *The Canine Good Citizen: Every Dog Can Be One*, 2nd edition, Howell Book House, 1997.

National Breed Club

Every breed recognized by the American Kennel Club has a national (parent) club. National clubs are a great source of information on your breed. The web site for the Bichon Frise Club of America contains a wealth of information about the breed's history, health, care, training, the standard, and Bichon rescue. It can also help you find a Bichon club in your area.

Bichon Frise Club of America
Joanne Styles
Corresponding Secretary
32 Oak Street
Centereach, NY 11720
www.bichon.org

Registries

There are numerous all-breed, individual breed, canine sporting, and other special-interest dog clubs across the country. The American Kennel Club can provide you with a list of clubs in your area.

The American Kennel Club (AKC)
260 Madison Avenue
New York, NY 10016
(212) 696-8200
www.akc.org

Canadian Kennel Club (CKC)
89 Skyway Avenue
Etobicoke, Ontario
Canada M9W 6R4
(800) 250-8040 or (416) 675-5511
www.ckc.ca

United Kennel Club (UKC)
100 E. Kilgore Road
Kalamazoo, MI 49001-5598
(616) 343-9020
www.ukcdogs.com

Magazines

AKC Gazette
260 Madison Avenue
New York, NY 10016
(212) 696-8200
www.akc.org

The Bichon Frise Reporter
P.O. Box 6369, Department CP
Los Osos, CA 93412
(805) 528-2007
www.bichon.org/read.htm

Dog Fancy
P.O. Box 37185
Boone, IA 50037-0185
(800) 896-4939
www.dogfancy.com

Dog World
P.O. Box 37186
Boone, IA 50037-0186
(800) 896-4939
www.dogworldmag.com

Whole Dog Journal
P.O. Box 420234
Palm Coast, FL 32142-0234
(800) 829-9165
www.whole-dog-journal.com

Internet Resources

American Society for the Prevention of Cruelty to Animals
www.aspca.org
Features humane education and advocacy information, with a link to the ASPCA Poison Control Center.

American Veterinary Medical Association
www.avma.org
The latest veterinary medical news.

The Bichon Frise in Art
bingweb.binghamton.edu/~eshephar/bichoninart/bichoninart.html
A wonderful resource of Bichon-type dogs in artwork from the fifth century B.C. through the twentieth century is compiled by Edward J. Shephard Jr. on this web site. This online exhibition has been wonderfully researched and documented and is a great historical resource.

Canine Freestyle Federation
www.canine-freestyle.com
This site is devoted to canine freestyle—dancing with your dog. There's information about freestyle events, tips, and even music to choose!

Delta Society
www.deltasociety.org
A great resource for anything interested in therapy or service dogs.

Dog Friendly
www.dogfriendly.com
Information about traveling with dogs, including guidebooks.

Foundation for Pet-Provided Therapy
www.loveonaleash.org
A service organization supporting pet-provided therapy.

Index

Photo Credits:

Kent Dannen: 4–5, 8–9, 13, 15, 18, 19, 24, 26, 28, 33, 41, 44, 45, 52, 54, 59, 61, 62, 66, 77, 78, 85, 89, 91, 92–93, 94, 118, 122, 125

Jean M. Fogle: 17, 21, 25, 55, 120,

Howell Book House: 10

Shell Styles: 1, 31, 35, 48, 50, 82, 114, 116, 123

Toni Tucker: 11, 30, 37, 40, 42–43, 53, 64, 65, 67, 69, 70, 71, 72, 83,